CliffsNotes®

HESI® A2 Science
CRAM PLAN®

MW00449590

CliffsNotes®

HESI® A2 Science
CRAM PLAN®

by

Michael Reid, MSN, RN, CCRN

Houghton Mifflin Harcourt
Boston • New York

About the Author

Michael Reid, MSN, RN, CCRN, is a critical care nurse in the Chicagoland area. He has worked for prestigious hospitals such as The Johns Hopkins Hospital and Northwestern Memorial Hospital. In addition to working in ICUs, he teaches nursing, NCLEX, and critical care. He wrote *CliffsNotes NCLEX Cram Plan* as well as numerous resources through his company (Nursology, The NCLEX Cure). He also develops educational technology for nursing and the NCLEX, including course curriculums and course development.

Dedication

Future nurses and healthcare workers; excellent job getting to this step in your future. The amount of work to succeed in this field is incredible. You can do it. I believe in you. Continue the journey and move our field forward. Best of luck!

To my mother and father, and Edson, whose support made this book possible. I love you all. Thank you!

Editorial

Executive Editor: Greg Tubach
Senior Editor: Christina Stambaugh
Production Editor: Jennifer Freilach
Copy Editor: Lynn Northrup
Technical Editors: Dr. Marcia Stout, DNP, and Jenna Duerst, RN
Proofreader: Susan Moritz

CliffsNotes® HESI® A2 Science Cram Plan®

Copyright © 2021 by Michael Reid
All rights reserved.

Library of Congress Control Number: 2020947699
ISBN: 978-0-358-21234-8 (pbk)

Printed in the United States of America
DOC 10 9 8 7 6 5 4 3 2 1

For information about permission to reproduce selections from this book, write to trade.permissions@hmhco.com or to Permissions, Houghton Mifflin Harcourt Publishing Company, 3 Park Avenue, 19th Floor, New York, New York 10016.

www.hmhbooks.com

Note: If you purchased this book without a cover, you should be aware that this book is stolen property. It was reported as "unsold and destroyed" to the publisher, and neither the author nor the publisher has received any payment for this "stripped book."

THE PUBLISHER AND THE AUTHOR MAKE NO REPRESENTATIONS OR WARRANTIES WITH RESPECT TO THE ACCURACY OR COMPLETENESS OF THE CONTENTS OF THIS WORK AND SPECIFICALLY DISCLAIM ALL WARRANTIES, INCLUDING WITHOUT LIMITATION WARRANTIES OF FITNESS FOR A PARTICULAR PURPOSE. NO WARRANTY MAY BE CREATED OR EXTENDED BY SALES OR PROMOTIONAL MATERIALS. THE ADVICE AND STRATEGIES CONTAINED HEREIN MAY NOT BE SUITABLE FOR EVERY SITUATION. THIS WORK IS SOLD WITH THE UNDERSTANDING THAT THE PUBLISHER IS NOT ENGAGED IN RENDERING LEGAL, ACCOUNTING, OR OTHER PROFESSIONAL SERVICES. IF PROFESSIONAL ASSISTANCE IS REQUIRED, THE SERVICES OF A COMPETENT PROFESSIONAL PERSON SHOULD BE SOUGHT. NEITHER THE PUBLISHER NOR THE AUTHOR SHALL BE LIABLE FOR DAMAGES ARISING HEREFROM. THE FACT THAT AN ORGANIZATION OR WEBSITE IS REFERRED TO IN THIS WORK AS A CITATION AND/OR A POTENTIAL SOURCE OF FURTHER INFORMATION DOES NOT MEAN THAT THE AUTHOR OR THE PUBLISHER ENDORSES THE INFORMATION THE ORGANIZATION OR WEBSITE MAY PROVIDE OR RECOMMENDATIONS IT MAY MAKE. FURTHER, READERS SHOULD BE AWARE THAT INTERNET WEBSITES LISTED IN THIS WORK MAY HAVE CHANGED OR DISAPPEARED BETWEEN WHEN THIS WORK WAS WRITTEN AND WHEN IT IS READ.

Trademarks: Cram Plan, CliffsNotes, the CliffsNotes logo, Cliffs, CliffsAP, CliffsComplete, CliffsQuickReview, CliffsStudySolver, CliffsTestPrep, CliffsNote-a-Day, cliffsnotes.com, and all related trademarks, logos, and trade dress are trademarks or registered trademarks of Houghton Mifflin Harcourt and/or its affiliates. HESI® is a registered trademark of Elsevier, Inc., which neither sponsors nor endorses this product. All other trademarks are the property of their respective owners. Houghton Mifflin Harcourt is not associated with any product or vendor mentioned in this book.

Table of Contents

Introduction

About the HESI Admission Assessment Exam (HESI A2)

HESI stands for Health Education Systems, Inc., with A2 standing for Admission Assessment. The HESI A2 has been used for years by nursing schools and other health fields as a tool to assess student readiness. Many schools use it as a benchmark for how well a student can be expected to perform in nursing school or higher education. The content on the HESI A2 involves a variety of topic areas, but most schools do not require every single one. Before you register for the HESI A2, make sure you understand which specific areas of the exam will be required by the school or schools to which you are applying. You do not want to miss any areas needed for an application.

The HESI A2 exam itself is written at a beginning-college-student level. Many topics are covered in high school courses. Whether you have taken advanced classes in high school or not, this book is an excellent review of the science portions for the exam.

The following table details the subject areas on the HESI A2. This book covers the four *science* areas specifically: biology, chemistry, anatomy and physiology, and physics. The full time available for the exam is typically 4 to 6 hours, depending on the total sections required. Time allotment for each of the science areas is typically 25 minutes, with physics typically 50 minutes. Time allowed is chosen by the school itself. Rarely do students run out of time. The questions are in multiple-choice format.

Topic	Total Number of Questions
Biology	25
Chemistry	25
Anatomy and Physiology	25
Physics	25
Vocabulary and General Knowledge	50
Reading Comprehension	47
Mathematics	50
Grammar	50

In addition to the above eight test areas for the HESI A2, there are two sections devoted to personality and learning style. The personality profile is 15 questions, and the learning style portion is 14 questions. These two areas are not scored.

About This Book

As mentioned above, this book covers the four HESI A2 science topics. I believe that any student who has basic knowledge of the science portions can easily use this book to brush up, prepare, and master the required knowledge to ace these sections on the HESI A2. If the school you are applying to requires portions not provided in this book, such as vocabulary or grammar, I recommend brushing up on those topics as well. The vocabulary section on the HESI A2, for example, is largely driven by medical terminology basics.

The four science areas presented in this book are as follows: *biology*, *chemistry*, *anatomy and physiology*, and *physics*. Each of the four review chapters contains a post-chapter practice quiz with answer explanations. These practice questions were written specifically at the HESI A2 level. At the end of the book are 50-question practice exams for the biology and the anatomy and physiology areas. I opted to not include practice exams for chemistry and physics, as they are less commonly required for nursing school applications.

Retaking the Exam

Although most students only have to take the HESI A2 one time, some students may want to take it a second time to improve their scores. Nursing schools typically accept the higher score and ignore the lower; most also consider a score in the 70%–80% range to be satisfactory. Individual schools will post any score requirements they may have.

A Note from the Author

Utilize the cram plan study calendars in Chapter 1 to guide you through your review of the content in this book. As you work through the chapters, you will see that the subject matter is presented in an easy-to-read and easy-to-absorb manner—a true "CliffsNotes" representation of the HESI A2 science areas. Take your time, and do not be discouraged if you do not recognize something right away. Most of this knowledge may have been presented in high school, but as anyone in education knows, getting the information to sink into the brain is a whole different matter.

Best of luck to you as you study through your specific cram plan in preparation for the HESI A2!

Michael Reid, MSN, RN, CCRN
Director of Nursing Development
Nursology & The NCLEX Cure
www.nursology.com

Chapter 1

Cram Plan Study Calendars

Determining Your HESI A2 Cram Plan

Take the following steps to determine which of the three cram plan study calendars best fits your needs:

1. Take the diagnostic test for each HESI A2 science section (physics excluded).
2. Use the answer key to find your baseline percentage.
3. Keep in mind additional HESI A2 topics that may not be in this book.
4. For each test area, check the box of the cram plan that works within your schedule: two-month, one-month, or one-week.

Your HESI A2 Cram Plan				
Test Area	**Your Score**	**Your Cram Plan**		
Biology		❏ Two-Month Cram Plan	❏ One-Month Cram Plan	❏ One-Week Cram Plan
Chemistry		❏ Two-Month Cram Plan	❏ One-Month Cram Plan	❏ One-Week Cram Plan
Anatomy and Physiology		❏ Two-Month Cram Plan	❏ One-Month Cram Plan	❏ One-Week Cram Plan
Physics	NA	❏ Two-Month Cram Plan	❏ One-Month Cram Plan	❏ One-Week Cram Plan

The cram plan calendars appear on the next few pages. Once you determine which cram plan calendar to follow for each test area, stick with it. If you choose a two-month or one-month cram plan calendar, you should have ample time to review all four science topics. If you choose a one-week cram plan calendar, you'll want to focus on the areas where your initial diagnostic test score was not in the 70%–80% range.

> Note: A 70%–80% performance is a common benchmark used by nursing schools.

Because the HESI A2 exam is completely dependent on which portions are required by your nursing school, an overall study plan can be difficult to assess. Keep in mind where your focus should be and plan accordingly. The cram plan calendars reflect the same strategy of attack; however, additional time means less rushing and more time for you to fully grasp a concept.

Given the briefness of the topics covered in this book, everything applicable should be plausibly covered in one month or more. If you have more time before your HESI A2, additional practice can be found online. Work at a pace that is comfortable for you.

On your final days before the HESI A2, follow what to do on pp. 4–5. There are some recommendations for final prep and what to do on the day of the exam.

Two-Month Cram Plan

Two-Month Cram Plan	

8 weeks before the exam	**Study Time:** 1–2 hours a day for 2–3 days
	❑ Read Chapter 5, "Biology Review."
	  ❑ Take end-of-chapter quiz.
	  ❑ Review quiz answers and explanations.
	  ❑ For any quiz questions that you answered incorrectly, review the appropriate section.

7 weeks before the exam	**Study Time:** 1–2 hours a day for 2–3 days
	❑ Read Chapter 6, "Chemistry Review."
	  ❑ Take end-of-chapter quiz.
	  ❑ Review quiz answers and explanations.
	  ❑ For any quiz questions that you answered incorrectly, review the appropriate section.

6 weeks before the exam	**Study Time:** 1–2 hours a day for 2–3 days
	❑ Read Chapter 7, "Anatomy and Physiology Review."
	  ❑ Take end-of-chapter quiz.
	  ❑ Review quiz answers and explanations.
	  ❑ For any quiz questions that you answered incorrectly, review the appropriate section.

5 weeks before the exam	**Study Time:** 1–2 hours a day for 2–3 days
	❑ Read Chapter 8, "Physics Review."
	  ❑ Take end-of-chapter quiz.
	  ❑ Review quiz answers and explanations.
	  ❑ For any quiz questions that you answered incorrectly, review the appropriate section.

4 weeks before the exam	**Study Time:** 1–2 hours
	❑ Take the "Biology Practice Exam" in Chapter 9.
	  ❑ Review answers and explanations.
	  ❑ For any test questions that you answered incorrectly, review the appropriate section in Chapter 5.

3 weeks before the exam	**Study Time:** 1–2 hours
	❑ Take the "Anatomy and Physiology Practice Exam" in Chapter 10.
	  ❑ Review answers and explanations.
	  ❑ For any test questions that you answered incorrectly, review the appropriate section in Chapter 7.

2 weeks before the exam	**Study Time:** 1–2 hours a day for 2–3 days
	❑ Chapter 5, "Biology Review" ❑ Chapter 6, "Chemistry Review"
	  ❑ Retake end-of-chapter quiz. ❑ Retake end-of-chapter quiz.
	  ❑ Review quiz answers and explanations. ❑ Review quiz answers and explanations.

1 week before the exam	**Study Time:** 1–2 hours a day for 2–3 days
	❑ Chapter 7, "Anatomy and Physiology Review" ❑ Chapter 8, "Physics Review"
	  ❑ Retake end-of-chapter quiz. ❑ Retake end-of-chapter quiz.
	  ❑ Review quiz answers and explanations. ❑ Review quiz answers and explanations.

Final days before the exam	**Study Time:** 1–2 hours a day for 2–3 days
	❑ Retake the "Biology Practice Exam" in Chapter 9.
	  ❑ Review answers and explanations.
	  ❑ For any test questions that you answered incorrectly, review the appropriate section in Chapter 5.
	❑ Retake the "Anatomy and Physiology Practice Exam" in Chapter 10.
	  ❑ Review answers and explanations.
	  ❑ For any test questions that you answered incorrectly, review the appropriate section in Chapter 7.

One-Month Cram Plan

One-Month Cram Plan	

4 weeks before the exam	**Study Time:** 2–3 hours a day for 2–3 days
	❏ Read Chapter 5, "Biology Review."
	    ❏ Take end-of-chapter quiz.
	    ❏ Review quiz answers and explanations.
	    ❏ For any quiz questions that you answered incorrectly, review the appropriate section.
	❏ Read Chapter 6, "Chemistry Review."
	    ❏ Take end-of-chapter quiz.
	    ❏ Review quiz answers and explanations.
	    ❏ For any quiz questions that you answered incorrectly, review the appropriate section.

3 weeks before the exam	**Study Time:** 2–3 hours a day for 2–3 days
	❏ Read Chapter 7, "Anatomy and Physiology Review."
	    ❏ Take end-of-chapter quiz.
	    ❏ Review quiz answers and explanations.
	    ❏ For any quiz questions that you answered incorrectly, review the appropriate section.
	❏ Read Chapter 8, "Physics Review."
	    ❏ Take end-of-chapter quiz.
	    ❏ Review quiz answers and explanations.
	    ❏ For any quiz questions that you answered incorrectly, review the appropriate section.

2 weeks before the exam	**Study Time:** 1–2 hours
	❏ Take the "Biology Practice Exam" in Chapter 9.
	    ❏ Review answers and explanations.
	    ❏ For any test questions that you answered incorrectly, review the appropriate section in Chapter 5.

1 week before the exam	**Study Time:** 1–2 hours
	❏ Take the "Anatomy and Physiology Practice Exam" in Chapter 10.
	    ❏ Review answers and explanations.
	    ❏ For any test questions that you answered incorrectly, review the appropriate section in Chapter 7.

Final days before the exam	**Study Time:** 1 hour a day for 2–3 days
	❏ Chapter 5, "Biology Review"
	    ❏ Retake end-of-chapter quiz.
	    ❏ Review quiz answers and explanations.
	❏ Chapter 6, "Chemistry Review"
	    ❏ Retake end-of-chapter quiz.
	    ❏ Review quiz answers and explanations.
	❏ Chapter 7, "Anatomy and Physiology Review"
	    ❏ Retake end-of-chapter quiz.
	    ❏ Review quiz answers and explanations.
	❏ Chapter 8, "Physics Review"
	    ❏ Retake end-of-chapter quiz.
	    ❏ Review quiz answers and explanations.

One-Week Cram Plan

One-Week Cram Plan	

7 days before the exam	**Study Time:** 3–4 hours
	❏ Read Chapter 5, "Biology Review."
	  ❏ Take end-of-chapter quiz.
	  ❏ Review quiz answers and explanations.
	  ❏ For any quiz questions that you answered incorrectly, review the appropriate section.
	❏ Read Chapter 6, "Chemistry Review."
	  ❏ Take end-of-chapter quiz.
	  ❏ Review quiz answers and explanations.
	  ❏ For any quiz questions that you answered incorrectly, review the appropriate section.

6 days before the exam	**Study Time:** 3–4 hours
	❏ Read Chapter 7, "Anatomy and Physiology Review."
	  ❏ Take end-of-chapter quiz.
	  ❏ Review quiz answers and explanations.
	  ❏ For any quiz questions that you answered incorrectly, review the appropriate section.
	❏ Read Chapter 8, "Physics Review."
	  ❏ Take end-of-chapter quiz.
	  ❏ Review quiz answers and explanations.
	  ❏ For any quiz questions that you answered incorrectly, review the appropriate section.

5 days before the exam	**Study Time:** 1–2 hours
	❏ Take the "Biology Practice Exam" in Chapter 9.
	  ❏ Review answers and explanations.
	  ❏ For any test questions that you answered incorrectly, review the appropriate section in Chapter 5.

4 days before the exam	**Study Time:** 1–2 hours
	❏ Take the "Anatomy and Physiology Practice Exam" in Chapter 10.
	  ❏ Review answers and explanations.
	  ❏ For any test questions that you answered incorrectly, review the appropriate section in Chapter 7.

Final days before the exam	**Study Time:** 1 hour a day for 1–2 days
	❏ Chapter 5, "Biology Review"
	  ❏ Retake end-of-chapter quiz.
	  ❏ Review quiz answers and explanations.
	❏ Chapter 6, "Chemistry Review"
	  ❏ Retake end-of-chapter quiz.
	  ❏ Review quiz answers and explanations.
	❏ Chapter 7, "Anatomy and Physiology Review"
	  ❏ Retake end-of-chapter quiz.
	  ❏ Review quiz answers and explanations.
	❏ Chapter 8, "Physics Review"
	  ❏ Retake end-of-chapter quiz.
	  ❏ Review quiz answers and explanations.

The Night Before and the Day of the HESI A2

The Night Before and the Day of the HESI A2	
The night before the exam	**What to do:** ❑ Do not do any heavy studying. If anything, skim through the review chapters for last-minute refreshers. ❑ Go to bed early, regardless of your exam time the next day. ❑ Do not drink alcohol or take any stimulants.
The day of the exam	**What to do:** ❑ Eat breakfast. ❑ Stay hydrated. ❑ Listen to classical music on the way to the HESI A2. Research shows that listening to classical music increases memory recall. ❑ Breathe deeply if you experience anxiety before or during the exam.

Chapter 2

Biology Diagnostic Test

This 15-question diagnostic test allows for a sense of personal weakness or strength in the biology area of the HESI A2. Remember, 70%–80% is the goal for each test area.

Note: This book does not include a diagnostic test for the physics area. It is rare for colleges to require physics for nursing students.

1 Ⓐ Ⓑ Ⓒ Ⓓ
2 Ⓐ Ⓑ Ⓒ Ⓓ
3 Ⓐ Ⓑ Ⓒ Ⓓ
4 Ⓐ Ⓑ Ⓒ Ⓓ
5 Ⓐ Ⓑ Ⓒ Ⓓ

6 Ⓐ Ⓑ Ⓒ Ⓓ
7 Ⓐ Ⓑ Ⓒ Ⓓ
8 Ⓐ Ⓑ Ⓒ Ⓓ
9 Ⓐ Ⓑ Ⓒ Ⓓ
10 Ⓐ Ⓑ Ⓒ Ⓓ

11 Ⓐ Ⓑ Ⓒ Ⓓ
12 Ⓐ Ⓑ Ⓒ Ⓓ
13 Ⓐ Ⓑ Ⓒ Ⓓ
14 Ⓐ Ⓑ Ⓒ Ⓓ
15 Ⓐ Ⓑ Ⓒ Ⓓ

15 Questions

Directions: Select the best answer choice for each question and mark it on the provided answer sheet.

1. Which of the following would you likely see on messenger RNA (mRNA), but not on DNA?

    A. Nucleic acids
    B. Amino acids
    C. Cytosine
    D. Uracil

2. What is the name of the process by which molecules move from a high concentration gradient to a lower concentration gradient?

    A. Osmosis
    B. Diffusion
    C. Solvency
    D. Adhesion

3. If a protein were catabolized, what would you likely find as a result of the reaction?

    A. Fatty acids
    B. Nucleic acids
    C. Amino acids
    D. Glucose

4. What do we call outward expressions of genetic traits, such as hair color and eye color?

    A. Phenotype
    B. Allele combinations
    C. Genotype
    D. Mutations

5. In regards to the classification of life on Earth (taxonomy), which of the following is the broadest category?

    A. Order
    B. Species
    C. Phylum
    D. Genus

6. A cell that is specialized in creating proteins would contain plenty of which organelle?

    A. Mitochondria
    B. Ribosomes
    C. Golgi apparatus
    D. DNA

7. When a cell reproduces and both daughter cells are identical to the mother cell, what type of cell reproduction would we call this?

   A. Sexual reproduction
   B. Gamete creation
   C. Binary fission
   D. Meiosis

8. How do prokaryotic organisms differ from eukaryotic organisms?

   A. Prokaryotic organisms' cells contain a nucleus with DNA.
   B. Prokaryotic organisms reproduce sexually.
   C. Prokaryotic organisms' cells do not have a nucleus.
   D. Prokaryotic organisms are likely animals or plants.

9. In which of the following scenarios does an organism absorb carbon dioxide and release oxygen?

   A. A plant performing photosynthesis
   B. An animal performing anaerobic respiration
   C. An animal performing glycolysis
   D. A plant performing fermentation

10. The scientific method is an important part of our understanding of life and biology in general. Which of the following is the final step in this process?

    A. Observations
    B. Experiments
    C. Questions
    D. Conclusions

11. Humans have 46 chromosomes. How many chromosomes exist in the gametes of a human?

    A. 46
    B. 23
    C. 18
    D. 9

12. Which of the following describes water's natural ability to stick to itself?

    A. Adhesion
    B. Cohesion
    C. High specific heat
    D. Polarity

13. In what type of molecule would fatty acids likely reside?

    A. Proteins
    B. DNA
    C. Complex sugars
    D. Lipids

14. Protein molecules are vital to life. DNA carries the information to create a protein. What molecule assists in this process to transport the information?

    A. Glucose
    B. mRNA
    C. DNA polymerase
    D. Vacuoles

15. Moving large molecules through a cell membrane from a low concentration to a high concentration requires specialized transportation. Which molecule is required for this transportation to occur?

    A. ADP
    B. ATP
    C. NADH
    D. Pyruvate

Answer Key

1. D	4. A	7. C	10. D	13. D
2. B	5. C	8. C	11. B	14. B
3. C	6. B	9. A	12. B	15. B

Answer Explanations

1. **D.** The bases for DNA and RNA are the same, with the exception of uracil in RNA, choice D. Uracil takes the place of thymine, which exists on DNA. Nucleic acids (choice A) exist on both RNA and DNA; the "NA" stands for nucleic acids. Amino acids (choice B) are the building blocks for proteins. Cytosine (choice C) exists on both RNA and DNA.

2. **B.** Diffusion, simply put, is when things move from high to low concentration, choice B. That "thing" could really be anything. If water moves in this nature, you can call it diffusion, but a more accurate term would be osmosis. This question did not reference the movement of water; if it had, osmosis (choice A) would have been the best answer. Solvency (choice C) refers to something dissolving in water. Water may act as an adhesive (choice D) when it sticks to other types of molecules.

3. **C.** If you catabolize, or break down, a molecule, you will likely find the building blocks of that molecule; in the case of a protein, you will find amino acids, choice C. Fatty acids (choice A) are one of the building blocks of lipids. Nucleic acids (choice B) are the building blocks for DNA and RNA. Glucose (choice D) is a building block for larger more complex sugars, such as starch and cellulose.

4. **A.** Outward expressions of genetic traits, such as hair color and eye color, are phenotypes of an organism, choice A. Any trait that is observable is considered a phenotype. Genotype (choice C) is the genetic composition of the organism; it CANNOT be observed. Allele combinations (choice B) involve heterozygous or homozygous sets. Mutations (choice D) describe a change in the genetic make-up of the organism in general.

5. **C.** Kingdom is the broadest or most inclusive classification available for life; however, it is not among the answer choices. The second-most broad classification is phylum, choice C. The other answer choices are more specific than phylum. The full classification hierarchy is as follows:

$$\text{kingdom} \rightarrow \text{phylum} \rightarrow \text{class} \rightarrow \text{order} \rightarrow \text{family} \rightarrow \text{genus} \rightarrow \text{species}$$

6. **B.** Ribosomes, choice B, are largely responsible for the creation of proteins. Mitochondria (choice A) create energy in the form of ATP. A Golgi apparatus (choice C) is a transportation hub, sending proteins throughout the cell. DNA (choice D) carries genetic material. Understanding what individual organelles do in the cell is important. Be sure to have a solid understanding before taking the HESI A2.

7. **C.** This type of reproduction where the daughter cells are identical to the mother cell is called binary fission, choice C, or mitosis. Both make sense. In sexual reproduction (choice A), such as meiosis (choice D), daughter cells contain half of the information of the mother cell (haploid). Gamete creation (choice B) is another way of saying meiosis.

8. **C.** The hallmark difference between prokaryotic and eukaryotic organisms is that prokaryotic organisms' cells do not have a nucleus, choice C, or membrane-bound organelles. All of the other answer choices describe eukaryotic cells. Complex multicellular organisms, such as plants and animals, are all eukaryotic. Prokaryotic organisms are either bacteria or archaea.

9. **A.** The biological reaction of photosynthesis requires water and carbon dioxide. When light is added, the reaction creates glucose and oxygen. Therefore, choice A, a plant performing photosynthesis, is correct. An animal performing anaerobic respiration (choice B) would not release oxygen; in fact, the reaction occurs in the absence of oxygen. Glycolysis (choice C) is the catabolism of glucose into pyruvate. Fermentation (choice D) creates lactic acid and/or ethanol as a byproduct. Alcohol fermentation is more common in organisms (yeast).

10. **D.** Drawing conclusions, choice D, is the final step in the scientific process. Upon conclusions, others should be able to follow the exact experiment and come to the exact same conclusions. If this does not happen, the experiment may be flawed. Identifying a question (choice C) is the first step, followed by a hypothesis, experiments (choice B), observations (choice A), and conclusions.

11. **B.** Gametes are haploid cells. If humans have 46 chromosomes, a gamete contains 23 chromosomes, choice B (haploid). Haploid simply means half, as many organisms have different amounts of chromosomes. For example, a chicken has 78 chromosomes, so its gametes would contain 39 chromosomes. The other answer choices do not reflect a genetic possibility in humans.

12. **B.** Cohesion, choice B, describes water's affinity for sticking to itself, whereas adhesion (choice A) describes the ability to stick to other things. Water has a high specific heat (choice C), meaning it takes more energy to increase the temperature of water compared to that of other substances. Think about large bodies of water like the Great Lakes. It takes a very long time and large environmental input to change the lakes' temperatures. Water's polarity (choice D) is best described by the types of bonds it creates (covalent).

13. **D.** Make sure to understand macromolecules and the components that created them. Fatty acids reside in fats/lipids, choice D. Proteins (choice A) are made up of amino acids. DNA (choice B) is made up of nucleic acids. Complex sugars (choice C) are made up of glucose.

14. **B.** DNA cannot leave the nucleus, so the information carried on it must be converted into another form. This is where RNA comes in. DNA translates into mRNA (messenger RNA), choice B. The mRNA leaves the nucleus and arrives at the ribosomes to translate the message and create proteins. Glucose (choice A) and vacuoles (choice D) do not carry genetic information. DNA polymerase (choice C) is an enzyme that aids in the replication of DNA itself, not in the transportation of information.

15. **B.** Active transport requires energy to move large molecules across the cell membrane. ATP (adenosine triphosphate) is the source of this energy, choice B. Smaller molecules and water can move by diffusion and osmosis. Active transport is also commonly required when pushing molecules against the gradient, such as a move from low to high concentration. ADP (choice A) is the inactivated version of ATP; it needs cellular respiration to convert back to ATP. NADH (choice C) and pyruvate (choice D) are utilized in the citric acid cycle to create more ATP.

Chapter 3

Chemistry Diagnostic Test

This 15-question diagnostic test allows for a sense of personal weakness or strength in the chemistry area of the HESI A2. Remember, 70%–80% is the goal for each test area.

Note: This book does not include a diagnostic test for the physics area. It is rare for colleges to require physics for nursing students.

1. (A) (B) (C) (D)
2. (A) (B) (C) (D)
3. (A) (B) (C) (D)
4. (A) (B) (C) (D)
5. (A) (B) (C) (D)

6. (A) (B) (C) (D)
7. (A) (B) (C) (D)
8. (A) (B) (C) (D)
9. (A) (B) (C) (D)
10. (A) (B) (C) (D)

11. (A) (B) (C) (D)
12. (A) (B) (C) (D)
13. (A) (B) (C) (D)
14. (A) (B) (C) (D)
15. (A) (B) (C) (D)

15 Questions

Directions: Select the best answer choice for each question and mark it on the provided answer sheet.

1. Carbon is one of the most important elements for life. It is found in countless compounds, from the food you eat to the air you exhale from your lungs. How many protons does carbon have? (Utilize the periodic table on p. 158.)

    A. 6
    B. 12
    C. 14
    D. 22

2. The reaction shown below is the breakdown of water into hydrogen and oxygen. By dropping a battery into water, you can observe this reaction, called electrolysis of water. The bubbling is a result of the released hydrogen atoms.

$$2\ H_2O \rightarrow 2H_2\ (g) + O_2(g)$$

    What type of reaction is this?

    A. Synthesis
    B. Decomposition
    C. Combustion
    D. Single replacement

3. Which of the following numbers displayed using scientific notation reflects the number 480,000?

    A. 4.8×10^{-5}
    B. 4.8×10^{5}
    C. 0.48×10^{6}
    D. 480×10^{4}

4. There are roughly 20 amino acids that are crucial to human life. In which of the following would you likely find amino acids?

    A. DNA
    B. Albumin
    C. Starch
    D. Cholesterol

5. If a healthcare worker were to administer 5,000 mcg of a medication, which of the following values is a correct conversion of the dose of medication?

    A. 10 kg
    B. 1 g
    C. 1 mg
    D. 5 mg

6. Which of the following combinations of traits correctly identifies an acid?

    A. Has increased levels of hydrogen and a pH less than 7
    B. Has decreased levels of hydrogen and a pH less than 7
    C. Has increased levels of hydrogen and a pH greater than 7
    D. Has decreased levels of hydrogen and a pH greater than 7

7. What is the oxidation state of the carbon atom in methane, CH_4?

    A. −4
    B. −2
    C. +2
    D. +4

8. At what degree Celsius does water freeze?

    A. −32
    B. 0
    C. 32
    D. 98.6

9. While useful for many things in the human body, cholesterol can also be harmful and lead to plaque build-up in arteries and veins. What type of molecule is cholesterol?

    A. Lipid
    B. Polysaccharide
    C. Enzyme
    D. Amino acid

10. A pentose, a 5-carbon chain, is commonly found in what type of compound?

    A. Starch
    B. Glycerol
    C. Amino acids
    D. All carbon-containing molecules

11. Carbon-14 is a radioactive isotope commonly used for carbon dating. How many neutrons does carbon-14 have?

   A.   0
   B.   6
   C.   8
   D.   14

12. Which of the following bonds is weakest?

   A.   Ionic
   B.   Covalent
   C.   Dipole interactions
   D.   Double

13. Which of the following types of matter have items very tightly packed together?

   A.   Gases
   B.   Plasma
   C.   Liquids
   D.   Solids

14. Sodium chloride, a common solution given intravenously (IV) to replenish a patient's fluids, is given the name "solution" because of what trait?

   A.   It is a heterogeneous mixture.
   B.   It is a homogeneous mixture.
   C.   The particles in the mixture do not spread out evenly.
   D.   "Solution" commonly describes a suspension.

15. If a disaccharide is split into two separate molecules, what are these molecules called?

   A.   Monosaccharide
   B.   Polysaccharide
   C.   Starch
   D.   Sucrose

Answer Key

1. A	4. B	7. A	10. A	13. D
2. B	5. D	8. B	11. C	14. B
3. B	6. A	9. A	12. C	15. A

Answer Explanations

1. **A.** The proton and electron number of any given element is the atomic number on the periodic table. The atomic number of carbon is 6; therefore, it contains 6 protons, choice A, and 6 electrons. This allows the neutral charge. The other answer choices do not reflect this. (Note: Atoms do not *always* contain the same number of electrons and protons, although this state is common.)

2. **B.** Decomposition, choice B, describes the breakdown of a molecule into smaller parts, in this case to hydrogen and oxygen atoms. The reaction shown in the question is already balanced. As you can see, oxygen is shown as a product of O_2. This is because oxygen, along with hydrogen, nitrogen, and a few others, is a diatomic molecule.

   Synthesis (choice A) is the building of a molecule from smaller parts; it's the opposite of decomposition. Combustion (choice C) is the breakdown of hydrocarbons, like CH_4 (methane) with added oxygen; the products are carbon dioxide and water. A single replacement (choice D) would show the movement of one reactant by the other; think of it as the bumping of one component of the reaction for another.

3. **B.** The formula for scientific notation is $C \times 10^n$, where C is the coefficient and n is the exponent. To form the coefficient, take the number provided, 480,000, and move the decimal place until you have a number between 1 and 10. For 480,000, the coefficient is 4.8. The power of 10 indicates how many places you moved the decimal. In this case, you moved the decimal 5 places. Therefore, in scientific notation, 480,000 is 4.8×10^5, choice B.

   Because the decimal is moved 5 places to the left to form the coefficient, the exponent is positive. A negative exponent indicates that the decimal point was moved to the right to form the coefficient. Choice A, 4.8×10^{-5}, is the scientific notation for 0.000048.

4. **B.** Amino acids are the building blocks of proteins. Albumin, choice B, is the only protein among the answer choices. DNA (choice A) is a nucleic acid, commonly containing sugar, phosphates, and base pairs. Starch (choice C) is a complex carbohydrate. Cholesterol (choice D) is a type of lipid.

5. **D.** One microgram (mcg) equals 0.001 milligram (mg). Therefore, 5,000 mcg = 5 mg, choice D. Moving throughout the metric system can be difficult for those who are not well versed in using it. Every decimal space moved comes to 10. Microgram is to the negative 6th power. Milligram is to the negative 3rd power. In this example, the three zeros are dropped. Make sure you know the most commonly used conversions in chemistry and science listed in this book. The other answer choices do not reflect a correct conversion.

6. **A.** As hydrogen levels increase, a substance becomes more acidic. As hydrogen levels decrease, a substance becomes more basic. A pH of 7 is neutral. A pH less than 7 is acidic, and a pH above 7 is basic. Therefore, increased levels of hydrogen and a pH less than 7, choice A, indicate an acid.

7. **A.** For the sake of HESI A2, know that hydrogen will always have an oxidation number of +1. CH_4 has four hydrogen atoms coming to a positive charge of +4. Molecules must remain neutral; therefore, in this example, carbon has a negative charge of –4, choice A.

   Finding the oxidation number can often be tricky because it depends on the molecule in question. Hydrogen always has a +1 charge. Oxygen has a –2 charge. Chlorine has a –1 charge. Utilizing this common knowledge, the molecules provided can be worked out.

8. **B.** Water freezes at 0 degrees Celsius, choice B (and at 32 degrees Fahrenheit, choice C). The question asks for the answer in Celsius, not Fahrenheit, so choice C is incorrect. Choice A, −32 degrees Celsius, does not reflect a commonly used degree. Choice D, 98.6, reflects a normal human body temperature in Fahrenheit.

9. **A.** Cholesterol is a type of lipid, choice A. A good trick for nomenclature is to recognize the suffix "sterol." All sterols are a type of lipid. Cholesterol is important in creating the cell membrane of all eukaryotes. We call it a phospholipid bilayer. Polysaccharides (choice B) are a type of sugar. The word "saccharide" is actually derived from the Latin word for "sugar." Enzymes (choice C) typically end with the suffix "ase," such as amylase (a digestive enzyme). Amino acids (choice D) are the building blocks of proteins.

10. **A.** Pentoses are 5-carbon chain monosaccharides. They are found in sugars, such as starch, choice A, or cellulose. Glycerol (choice B) is a polyol compound found in lipids. Amino acids (choice C) are found in proteins; they do not contain pentoses. Carbon is found in all organic compounds, but that does not necessarily mean they are 5-carbon chain-containing compounds, eliminating choice D.

11. **C.** Carbon typically has 6 protons, 6 neutrons, and 6 electrons, with 4 of the electrons in the outer valence shell. In carbon-14, however, with 14 being the total mass of the atom, there are 8 neutrons, choice C. Electron mass is negligible and therefore does not influence the atomic mass. With that knowledge, remember any changes to atomic mass will be manipulated by neutron count. Essentially it creates a simple math problem: 14 (mass) − 6 (proton count) = 8 neutron count.

12. **C.** Generally speaking, the more electrons that are involved in a bond, the stronger the bond. Dipole interactions do not involve electrons in a bond. The interaction occurs when a negative side of a molecule interacts with a positive side of another, and so forth. Therefore, there is no actual bond in a dipole interaction and it is quite weak, choice C. Covalent bonds (choice B) are the strongest.

13. **D.** Solids, choice D, are the most tightly packed of all states of matter. The atoms in solids are typically arranged in a fixed shape and do not move. In liquids (choice C), atoms are fairly close together and freely move around. In gases (choice A), atoms are far apart. Plasma (choice B) is not "technically" a defined state of matter, although some consider it the fourth state of matter. Plasma is a very hot ionized gas. A good example of where stellar plasma could be found is the Sun.

14. **B.** Only a homogeneous mixture, choice B, could potentially be described as a solution. If a solution is of a water solvent, it is called an aqueous solution, such as the aqueous humor of the eyeball. A heterogeneous mixture (choice A) is any mixture that is not uniform or completely dissolvable (e.g., oil and water). Particles that do not spread out evenly (choice C) would be a heterogeneous mixture as well as a suspension (choice D).

15. **A.** Nomenclature in chemistry typically has a basis in Latin—"mono" for one, "di" for two, "tri" for three, and so forth. A disaccharide contains two separate monosaccharides, choice A. An oligo-saccharide contains anywhere between three and six monosaccharides. Polysaccharides (choice B) contain numerous monosaccharides. Starch (choice C) is a type of polysaccharide. Sucrose (choice D) is an example of a disaccharide.

Chapter 4

Anatomy and Physiology Diagnostic Test

This 15-question diagnostic test allows for a sense of personal weakness or strength in the anatomy and physiology area of the HESI A2. Remember, 70%–80% is the goal for each test area.

Note: This book does not include a diagnostic test for the physics area. It is rare for colleges to require physics for nursing students.

1. Ⓐ Ⓑ Ⓒ Ⓓ
2. Ⓐ Ⓑ Ⓒ Ⓓ
3. Ⓐ Ⓑ Ⓒ Ⓓ
4. Ⓐ Ⓑ Ⓒ Ⓓ
5. Ⓐ Ⓑ Ⓒ Ⓓ

6. Ⓐ Ⓑ Ⓒ Ⓓ
7. Ⓐ Ⓑ Ⓒ Ⓓ
8. Ⓐ Ⓑ Ⓒ Ⓓ
9. Ⓐ Ⓑ Ⓒ Ⓓ
10. Ⓐ Ⓑ Ⓒ Ⓓ

11. Ⓐ Ⓑ Ⓒ Ⓓ
12. Ⓐ Ⓑ Ⓒ Ⓓ
13. Ⓐ Ⓑ Ⓒ Ⓓ
14. Ⓐ Ⓑ Ⓒ Ⓓ
15. Ⓐ Ⓑ Ⓒ Ⓓ

15 Questions

Directions: Select the best answer choice for each question and mark it on the provided answer sheet.

1. Nephrons that filter and clean out blood are part of what body system?

   A. Urinary system
   B. Filtering system
   C. Cardiovascular system
   D. Digestive system

2. Adipose tissue provides support and protection for the body and organs. What type of tissue is adipose tissue?

   A. Nervous
   B. Epithelial
   C. Connective
   D. Muscle

3. Bile is secreted to assist in the emulsification of fats through the gastrointestinal (GI) tract. In what anatomy and physiology classification does this process fall?

   A. Organ
   B. Cell
   C. System
   D. Tissue

4. Which of the following glands is responsible for the production of milk?

   A. Sebaceous gland
   B. Endocrine gland
   C. Pineal gland
   D. Sudoriferous gland

5. Which of the following combinations of enzymes and the materials they digest is correct?

   A. Amylase: starch
   B. Lipase: proteins
   C. Protease: fatty acids
   D. Amylase: amino acids

6. Schwann cells encase, conduct, and regenerate cells. Where are these cells found in the human body?

   A. Digestive system
   B. Nervous system
   C. Reproductive system
   D. Integumentary system

7. In what area of the human body does the heart exist?

   A.   Mediastinum
   B.   Pleural cavity
   C.   Dorsal cavity
   D.   Peritoneum

8. What type of muscle is responsible for peristalsis in the intestines, aiding in the movement of chyme through the gastrointestinal (GI) tract?

   A.   Smooth muscle
   B.   Skeletal muscle
   C.   Cardiac muscle
   D.   Striated muscle

9. The pancreas releases the hormone glucagon when blood sugar is low. Which organ or gland does glucagon work on to release glucose?

   A.   Islets of Langerhans
   B.   Gallbladder
   C.   Adrenal gland
   D.   Liver

10. Which neurotransmitter is responsible for the movement of our muscles by motor neurons?

   A.   Dopamine
   B.   Acetylcholine
   C.   Serotonin
   D.   GABA

11. If a surgeon wanted to dissect something into two equal right and left portions, what anatomical plane would he or she be creating?

   A.   Frontal
   B.   Transverse
   C.   Parasagittal
   D.   Midsagittal

12. Melanocytes are known to have the potential to become an aggressive form of metastatic cancer. What is the role of melanocytes in healthy human beings?

   A.   Aid in vitamin D absorption
   B.   Produce keratin in skin
   C.   Protect skin from bacteria and pathogens
   D.   Produce pigment that gives skin its color

13. A primary care doctor has told you that your bones are done growing. What would the doctor be looking at to make this determination?

    A. The level of growth hormone in the blood
    B. The epiphyseal plate of the long bones
    C. The number of red blood cells in the blood
    D. The density of bone

14. In an anemic patient, not enough red blood cells (RBCs) are circulating to carry oxygen. What part of the body is responsible for the release of a hormone to stimulate more RBC production?

    A. The bones
    B. The kidneys
    C. The blood
    D. The spleen

15. Which of the following statements about human vasculature is correct?

    A. Arteries are thin and carry blood away from the heart.
    B. Arteries are elastic and carry blood toward the heart.
    C. Arteries are elastic and carry blood away from the heart.
    D. Arteries are muscular and carry mostly deoxygenated blood.

Answer Key

1. A	4. D	7. A	10. B	13. B
2. C	5. A	8. A	11. D	14. B
3. C	6. B	9. D	12. D	15. C

Answer Explanations

1. **A.** Nephrons are part of the urinary system, choice A. "Neph" as a medical term means kidney. Nephrons survive inside kidneys, where there are more than 1 million nephrons in each kidney. Inside the nephron is the glomerulus, which is responsible for filtering and cleaning out the blood. The filtered-out product is then urinated out of the body.

   The filtering system (choice B) is not a real system; it does not exist. The cardiovascular system (choice C) pumps blood throughout the body via the heart and blood vessels. The digestive system (choice D) digests and absorbs food and nutrients. Part of the digestive system, the liver, does in fact filter and clean out the blood, but in a different way. Nephrons do not survive inside the liver.

2. **C.** Adipose tissue is a type of specialized, loose connective tissue, choice C. Each of this tissue's balloon-type cells, called adipocytes, carries lipids or fat. Nervous tissue (choice A) is composed of neurons and glial cells. Epithelial tissue (choice B) lines our skin, mucous membranes, and organs, among other areas. Muscle tissue (choice D) gives our bodies the ability to move.

3. **C.** While the liver, an organ, is responsible for the production of bile, and the gallbladder, also an organ, stores it, this question is discussing specifically the digestion of fats. In digestion, *emulsify* means to break down fats into smaller pieces so the surface area is larger. This process is discussing the digestive system as a whole, choice C, not just one organ (choice A). Certain cells (choice B) and tissues (choice D) produce bile; they are called hepatocytes, which make up liver tissue.

4. **D.** The mammary glands are an enlarged and modified type of sudoriferous (sweat) glands, choice D; these glands are characteristic of mammals. These exocrine glands produce milk in clustered areas that resemble grapes. Sebaceous glands (choice A) secrete sebum (oil) to the skin. Endocrine glands (choice B) resemble glands that release their hormones to the inside ("endo") of the body, not the outside ("exocrine"). The pineal gland (choice C) resides in the brain and regulates melatonin for sleep.

5. **A.** Amylases are responsible for the breakdown of complex carbohydrates, such as starches, choice A. They digest down to smaller carbs, such as monosaccharides and disaccharides. Lipases (choice B) break down fats to fatty acids and monoglycerides, not proteins. Proteases (choice C) break down proteins into smaller peptides and amino acids, not fatty acids. Amylase does not break down amino acids (choice D).

6. **B.** Schwann cells, also called neurolemmocytes, can be myelinated or unmyelinated throughout the nervous system, choice B. They are most common in the peripheral nervous system. Schwann cells are not found in the digestive (choice A), reproductive (choice C), or integumentary (choice D) system.

7. **A.** The heart is located in the mediastinum, choice A. The mediastinum, Latin for "midway," lies in the center of the thoracic cavity, which also lies inside the ventral cavity. The pleural cavity (choice B) holds the lungs. The dorsal cavity (choice C) holds the brain and spinal cord. The peritoneum (choice D) holds most of the abdominal organs except for the kidneys and a few others; the kidneys are retroperitoneal.

8. **A.** Smooth muscle, choice A, is responsible for the movement of chyme through the GI tract. This movement is called peristalsis, a wavelike action of the hollow tube. Smooth muscle is also present in many other parts of the human body, including blood vessels and arrector pili muscles, which cause goosebumps on the skin. Skeletal muscle (choice B) helps us move our bodies, from walking to flipping the pages of this book. Skeletal muscle is also striated (choice D). Smooth muscle in this sense would be called "non-striated." Cardiac muscle (choice C) exists in the myocardium of the heart, facilitating the pumping of blood.

9. **D.** While glucagon is released by alpha cells inside the Islets of Langerhans (choice A), the end purpose of glucagon is to stimulate the liver, choice D, to release glucose. The gallbladder (choice B) holds bile produced by the liver and does not directly regulate blood glucose. The adrenal glands (choice C) may indirectly affect blood sugar at certain times, such as a "fight-or-flight" response, but it is not the result of glucagon.

10. **B.** Acetylcholine, choice B, is largely responsible for communicating signals from the brain through motor neurons to our muscles. It also functions to communicate to glandular tissue. Dopamine (choice A), serotonin (choice C), and GABA (choice D) are often referred to as the major neurotransmitters responsible for mood.

11. **D.** A midsagittal or longitudinal plane, choice D, dissects the body into equal left and right portions. If the right and left portions are unequal, it is called a parasagittal plane (choice C). A frontal plane (choice A) dissects the body into ventral (front) and dorsal (back) portions. A transverse plane (choice B), also called an axial plane, dissects the body into head and tail portions.

12. **D.** Melanocytes produce a pigment called melanin, which gives skin its color, choice D. They exist in the epidermis of human skin among other places. They indeed have the potential to become cancerous, something you will learn more about in nursing school. Keratinocytes, not melanocytes, produce the protein keratin in the skin, hair, nails, etc., making choice B incorrect. Melanocytes do not aid in vitamin D absorption, making choice A incorrect. The process by which vitamin D is synthesized is rather complicated and unneeded for the HESI A2. Very simply, the Sun's ultraviolet rays react with cholesterol in skin cells, allowing vitamin D3 (cholecalciferol) synthesis to occur. The skin itself is what protects the body from bacteria, pathogens, and invaders, eliminating choice C. The integumentary system as a whole is the body's first line of defense.

13. **B.** The epiphyseal plate, or growth plate, is originally cartilage in childhood and the growing years. The cartilage turns to bone at a certain point, ending the growth of the body. By looking at the epiphyseal plate, choice B, this determination can be made. Growth hormone (choice A) continues to be produced into adulthood, but for other purposes, such as muscle and bone development. The number of red blood cells (RBCs, choice C) does not correlate to growth in children to adulthood. RBCs carry oxygen. The density of bone (choice D) would not determine growth; some bone is not dense to begin with, such as spongy bone. Density is oftentimes looked at later in life for conditions like osteoporosis.

14. **B.** When the number of RBCs decreases in the blood, the kidneys, choice B, release a hormone called erythropoietin. This hormone stimulates erythropoiesis, or the production of RBCs. If a patient has kidney disease, it is not uncommon for the patient to be anemic. The spleen (choice D) does not produce hormones to stimulate RBC production. The spleen does, however, filter out old or damaged RBCs when they need to be taken out of active circulation. The bones (choice A), especially spongy bone, is where RBC production occurs; bone does not release a hormone to act upon itself. The blood (choice C) also does not release hormones to stimulate RBC production.

15. **C.** Arteries are highly elastic, choice C, to allow for the sheer pressure from the blood being ejected out of the left ventricle (blood pressure). Arteries carry blood away from the heart, not toward it (choice B), specifically blood from the aorta, which in turn forks into multiple segments. Arteries are muscular, not thin (choice A). They carry mostly oxygenated blood, not deoxygenated blood (choice D), except for the pulmonary artery. Veins are typically thin.

Chapter 5

Biology Review

The biology section on the HESI A2 contains 25 questions.

Biology is the study of life and living organisms. It is the foundation for future study in nursing, spanning a multitude of areas such as anatomy, physiology, and pathophysiology. Knowledge of biology is crucial to your future success in nursing school and to the overall success of a scientific intellect. Everything you touch, feel, or experience that is alive is a part of biology, including yourself.

Classification of Life

Life on this planet is organized into categories. Regardless of the organism, it falls into this system one way or another, including you, the *Homo sapien*. As the list goes downward, classification becomes smaller in number and more specific. For example, the phylum Chordata Vertebrata includes any type of animal with a spinal cord (e.g., birds, fish), but the class Mammalia narrows it down to animals that give birth to live young (e.g., whales, dogs, humans).

1. Kingdom
2. Phylum
3. Class
4. Order
5. Family
6. Genus
7. Species

Example: *Homo sapiens*/Humans

Animalia → Chordata Vertebrata → Mammalia → Primate → Hominidae → Homo → Sapien

HESI Tip: *Species* classification is the most specific category. A species may procreate and expand their size via reproduction. Kingdom classification is the most broad or inclusive category.

Scientific Method

Experimentation requires conditions that ensure results are factual and true. As is true with science pertinent to our own lives, there are times people present information as fact without proof. The purpose of the scientific method is to ensure that the research or hypothesis can be repeated by anyone with the same result recurring. False information does not repeat. The method is as follows:

1. Identify a problem or question.
2. Form a hypothesis.
3. Perform experiments or tests.
4. Observe the results.
5. Evaluate and form conclusions.

Example: *Peer Review Research*

An example would be a double-blind study. When even the researchers do not know a variable going into the research, it is difficult for people to say afterward that there was undue influence affecting the outcome. Remember, the point of the scientific method is for others to be able to repeat the research or hypothesis and get the same outcome. There must be no bias or outside influence.

Water (H_2O)

Water is necessary for life to exist. A fair question would be why. All life on this planet interacts with water to some degree. There are many qualities of water that make it a valuable molecule for living things to perform basic functions, one aspect being that water is liquid at room temperature. Water moves easily when it is liquid. Even in the harshest conditions on Earth, if water exists, life has been found.

Example: *Extremophiles*

Extremophiles survive in hydrothermal vents in the ocean, where temperatures can reach up to 176 degrees Fahrenheit.

Water has the following noteworthy qualities:

1. Polarity
   - Covalent bonds to hydrogen give water its polarity.
   - Hydrogen atoms easily bond to other molecules.
   - Universal solvent; almost everything dissolves in water
   - Allows water molecules to move easily between membranes
2. High specific heat
   - Water does not easily change temperature.
   - Latent heat also high (solid to liquid, liquid to gas)
3. Cohesive
   - Water sticks to itself.
4. Adhesive
   - Water sticks to other substances.

Organic Compounds

There are many names for organic compounds—macromolecules, biochemical compounds, biopolymers. These names describe large combinations of molecules important to life. All life interacts with these molecules to some degree. Slight crossover between biology and chemistry may exist. Many students learn about organic compounds in a class specifically developed for the topic: biochemistry.

Carbohydrates
   - Structural format:
     o CH_2O
     o Carbon and water
     o Aid in DNA/RNA structure

- Monosaccharide
  - Glucose (simple sugar)
  - Most common form of energy
  - One monomer sequence
- Polysaccharides
  - Starch and cellulose
  - Large and complex sugars (polymer)
  - Storage of energy
- Glycolysis
  - Breakdown of glucose
  - Enzyme catalyzed
  - Use of pyruvate to form ATP and NADH (energy)

Lipids (Fats)

- Structural format:
  - Multiple carbon/hydrogen bonds (C-H)
  - Take many forms (e.g., fatty acids, cholesterol)
  - Storage of energy and structural components anatomically (insulation)
- Hydrophobic
  - Repel water (do not mix well)
- Fats (glycerides)
  - Triglycerides (tri = 3 chains)
  - Glycerol (the head) with fatty acid chains (the tails)
  - Saturated
    - No double bonds in tails
    - Linear appearance
    - Solid
  - Unsaturated
    - Double bonds in tails
    - Broken appearance
    - Liquid
- Phospholipids
  - Contain phosphate group bonded to lipids
  - Used in cell membrane structure (phospholipid bilayer)
- Steroids
  - Four-ring molecules
  - Send signals (steroid hormones)
  - Used in both animals (testosterone, cortisol) and plants

Proteins

- Structural format:
  - Amino acid combinations formed by amide bonds
  - Many peptides form together (polypeptides)
  - Example: Hemoglobin
- Enzymes
  - Catalytic (break down)
  - End in "ase," such as amyl**ase** and lip**ase** (human digestion)
- Condensation reactions:
  - Cause release of water
  - Create large polymers (peptides)
- Hydrolysis reactions:
  - Cause absorption of water
  - Break down peptides

Nucleic Acids

- Store information in the DNA of all life
- Store energy in the form of adenosine triphosphate (ATP)
- Nucleotides
  - Monomer unit of DNA/RNA (polymer)
- Nitrogenous bases
  - Created by breakdown of nucleosides
  - Thymine, adenine, guanine, cytosine
- RNA/DNA
  - Nucleic acid polymers
  - Phosphodiester bonds join nucleotides together.
- Nitrogen fixation
  - Necessary for life
  - Used to create organic compounds that contain nitrogen (amino acids, proteins)

HESI Tip: Having a general understanding of names for some of the most common organic compounds is smart. Some are listed above; some are not, such as keratin. Keratin is a very common protein found in our skin and hair. Deoxyribose nucleic acid is the large extended name for what most people know as DNA.

Metabolism

To sustain life, all living organisms must perform chemical reactions. Without these reactions, certain functions would cease to operate. Think about it like cooking. If you do not have the right ingredients, you will not get the desired end result. In this analogy, the ingredients to build molecules come from glucose, amino acids, fatty acids, and nucleotides. For every macromolecule discussed in the previous section, there is a series of metabolic pathways that explain it.

In the opposite direction, there are many metabolic pathways that break molecules down into smaller components. This makes them readily available for use by the organism.

Types of Reactions

- Catabolic: Releases energy when compounds are broken down
- Anabolic: Absorbs energy as compounds are created
- Endothermic: Absorbs heat
- Exothermic: Releases heat
- Condensation: Releases water
- Hydrolysis: Absorbs water

Catabolic Reactions

- Break down large molecules into small molecules
- Allow the body to create ATP from simple molecules
- Example: Starch (polysaccharide) to glucose (monosaccharide)
  o Glucose is vital to cell function.
- Example: Protein to amino acids

Anabolic Reactions

- Create large molecules from small molecules (biosynthesis)
- Utilize ATP to build up molecules
- Example: Liver creates glucose when blood sugar is low.

HESI Tip: Know the building blocks for macromolecules and the biological names used. A good way of thinking about it would be to ask questions such as "what makes up complex sugars" or "what makes up a protein." From there, catabolic or anabolic reactions make more sense.

The Cell

To understand cellular biology is to understand the beginning of life on this planet. All life contains cells. Cells are the smallest structural component of all organisms. They can take on many different forms, but the majority carry similar characteristics. A defining characteristic of all cells is that they contain DNA. What may change is the location of the DNA: prokaryotic versus eukaryotic, as described below.

Prokaryotic Cells	Eukaryotic Cells
- No nucleus	- Nucleus
- Generally simple	- Generally complex
- Contain no organelles	- Contain organelles
- Multiply by binary fission	- Multiply by mitosis
- Example: Bacteria (*escherichia coli*)	- Examples: Plants and animals

Another common way of differentiating between cells is animal versus plant. Both animal and plant cells are eukaryotic; however, some notable differences exist.

Plant Cells	Animal Cells
■ Cell wall	■ No cell wall
■ One large vacuole	■ Several small vacuoles
■ Chloroplasts	■ Lysosomes
o Used in photosynthesis	o Contain digestive enzymes
o Create ATP for plant cells	o Destroy invading viruses and bacteria

Organelles

- Nucleus
  - Contains DNA and chromosomes (genetic information)
  - Does not exist in red blood cells
- Mitochondria
  - Energy production (ATP)
  - Do not exist in bacteria
- Ribosomes
  - Create proteins from amino acids
  - Can be bound to endoplasmic reticulum or free floating
- Endoplasmic reticulum (ER)
  - Smooth ER breaks down molecules.
  - Rough ER (ribosomes attached) builds membrane and proteins.
- Golgi apparatus
  - Transports proteins throughout the cell
- Lysosomes
  - Break down sugars, fats, proteins, and nucleic acids
  - Utilize enzymes for reactions
- Vacuoles
  - Contain many different types of molecules
  - Transport waste, food, and water
  - May function by phagocytosis ("cell eating")
- Cytoplasm
  - The majority of space inside a cell
  - Contains cytosol and organelles (not the nucleus)
- Cellular membrane
  - Protection and structure of the cell
  - Constructed of phospholipid bilayer
  - Selectively chooses what may enter or leave the cell (transport proteins)
  - Integrated proteins act as active transport mechanisms (ATP required)

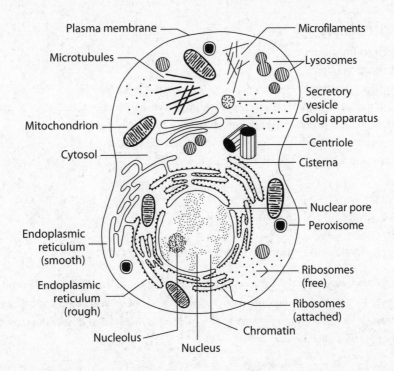

HESI Tip: Passive transport by the cell membrane requires no energy. This action occurs when molecules move from a higher concentration to a lower concentration (e.g., osmosis with water or diffusion). Active transport or facilitated diffusion requires energy in the form of ATP and the utilization of a transport protein in the membrane. The protein pushes the molecule to a place of higher concentration. Typically, larger molecules require active transport.

Cellular Respiration

The goal of cellular respiration is the creation of energy in the form of adenosine triphosphate (ATP). ATP provides energy to living organisms for a multitude of processes such as muscle movement. The creation of ATP in the cell is accomplished by a pathway of reactions (oxidative and reductive); some pathways are more productive than others. Nicotinamide adenine dinucleotide (NADH) is an important molecule in cellular respiration; it produces 3 ATP in the electron transport chain.

Anaerobic Respiration

- Does not utilize oxygen
- Produces far fewer ATP than aerobic respiration
- Produces 2 ATP molecules

Aerobic Respiration

- Requires oxygen to function
- Complex, but more effective
- Glycolysis produces pyruvate.
- Pyruvate begins the citric acid cycle (Krebs cycle) inside the mitochondria.
- Electron transport chain produces large amounts of ATP and water.
- These reactions create carbon dioxide, water, and heat (byproducts).
- One glucose molecule creates 32 to 36 molecules of ATP.

Fermentation

- Creates ATP in the absence of oxygen
- Uses pyruvate
- Some animals use lactic acid and/or ethanol fermentation.

HESI Tip: Cellular respiration, especially the citric acid cycle (Krebs cycle), is incredibly complex and difficult to learn. It may be helpful to look at a diagram showing the entire process, but do not go overboard and believe the memorization of everything is necessary. The goal is understanding the molecules involved and how the process is driven. It also helps to study the chemical equation below.

$$C_6H_{12}O_6 + 6\,O_2 \rightarrow 6\,CO_2 + 6\,H_2O$$

Observe how carbon dioxide and water are the byproducts of this reaction, and how oxygen is required. Think about the human body; we breathe in oxygen and breathe out carbon dioxide. This is part of our metabolism and a very basic function of the human body and many organisms.

Photosynthesis

The basic premise of photosynthesis is the creation of energy by utilizing light, most commonly from the Sun. The light is absorbed by plant proteins that contain chlorophyll, a pigment molecule residing in chloroplast organelles. Photosynthesis is the primary source of energy for plants, algae, and other organisms on Earth. These organisms, in turn, sustain other life by releasing oxygen as waste.

Photosynthesis can be thought of as the reverse of cellular respiration. Photosynthesis creates glucose from water, carbon dioxide, and light. These organisms then use the glucose for their functions.

Glucose Production

- Sugar is made in photosynthesis by using the Calvin cycle (a type of carbon fixation).
- The glucose is either stored or used for the creation of ATP.

Cyanobacteria

- Bacteria that use photosynthesis

Thylakoids

- Found inside chloroplasts
- Disc-like structure where photosynthesis occurs
- Photosystems of proteins exist here to perform vital functions of photosynthesis.

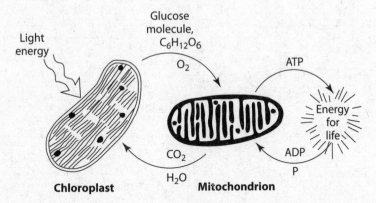

Cellular Reproduction

All life has to be replenished on a cellular level. Whether the organism is unicellular, such as bacteria, or multicellular, such as a human, cells must replicate and replace. A good example is your skin. Every cell that you see on your skin is already keratinized and dead; the basal cells underneath must replicate and replenish constantly. Different types of cells have different cell cycles, but replication is a must when cells are reproducing, old, or no longer serving a purpose.

Asexual Reproduction

- Binary fission
  - Common in bacteria
  - Daughter cells identical to parent cell
- Mitosis
  - Daughter cells identical to parent cell
  - Five-stage process of cell division:
    - *Prophase:* Chromosomes separate
    - *Prometaphase:* Chromosomes attach to spindle fibers
    - *Metaphase:* Alignment along metaphase plate (center of cell)
    - *Anaphase:* Chromosomes begin to separate
    - *Telophase:* Chromosomes are on different sides
- Cytokinesis
  - Process after mitosis
  - Cell splits into two

- Chromatids
  - Identical sister pieces of the chromosome
  - Connected at centromere
  - Chromosome looks like an "X" at this point.

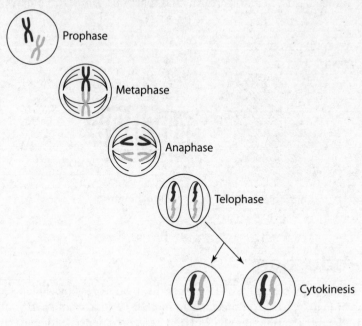

Ploidy

- Haploid
  - One chromosome set per cell
  - Gamete cells in humans
- Diploid
  - Two chromosome sets per cell
  - All other cells in humans (not gametes)

Sexual Reproduction

- Meiosis
  - Meiosis I and meiosis II (two stages—cell splits twice)
  - Two stages to create gametes (haploid)
  - Creates genetic material for sperm or eggs

DNA

Deoxyribose nucleic acid, or DNA for short, contains the genetic code for any organism. From *E. coli* bacteria, to palm trees, to an elephant, all of these organisms have complex genetic coding within their DNA. Some may be more complex than others, but all have DNA.

Structural Components

- Double helix structure
- Nucleotides make up DNA.
- Bases
  - Adenine (bonds with thymine)
  - Guanine (bonds with cytosine)
  - Cytosine (bonds with guanine)
  - Thymine (bonds with adenine)
  - Each base above bonds via hydrogen.
- DNA replication
  - Splits or unzips during replication
  - Helicases unzip the helix.
  - DNA polymerase, primase, and lipase assist in building.

HESI Tip: Studying the terminology can help drive understanding. For example, a term that ends in "ase" is likely to be an enzyme.

Protein Synthesis

- Transcription initiates protein synthesis.
- Messenger RNA (mRNA)
  - Created by transcription
  - Uracil replaces the base thymine in mRNA.
  - Each gene creates a unique mRNA.
  - mRNA moves to ribosomes.
- Codons
  - Three bases grouped together on mRNA
  - Requires an anticodon on transfer RNA (tRNA)
  - Amino acids exist on tRNA.
  - Stop codons end protein synthesis.

Genetics

Modern genetics is generally attributed to a man named Gregor Mendel. He was able to prove that certain traits (flower color) in peas followed familial lines, from generation to generation. Genetics today presents a somewhat different proposition with advancing technology, but the general premise is the same. If a species reproduces sexually, diversity exists.

Mendel's Laws

- Law of segregation: Each parent contributes half of genes.
- Law of independent assortment: Genes are selected at random.

Punnett Squares

- Display crossed alleles and potential genotypes and phenotypes
- Display probability of offspring outcomes
- Monohybrid cross
  - One allele trait cross
- Dihybrid cross
  - Two allele trait cross

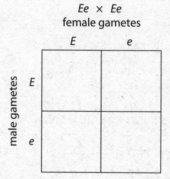

Genes

- A segment of DNA for one trait
- Autosomal: Exists on numbered chromosomes
- Sex-linked: Exists on X or Y chromosomes
- Polymorphic: Multiple combinations of alleles on a gene

Allele

- Dominant
  - Capitalized letters
  - Expressed in *HH* or *Hh*
- Recessive
  - Lowercase letters
  - Expressed in *hh*
- Homozygous
  - Same alleles
  - Examples: *hh* or *HH*
- Heterozygous
  - Different alleles
  - Example: *Hh*

Genotype
- The combination of genes
- Genotype may not be expressed (carriers)

Phenotype
- The expression of a trait
- What we can see
  o Examples: Hair color, eye color, etc.
- Dominance expressed regardless
  o Examples: *HH, Hh*
- Recessive expressed only when homozygous
  o Example: *hh*

HESI Tip: A dominant pattern or recessive pattern is also termed a "pattern of inheritance."

Mutations
- May lead to good (beneficial) or bad (harmful) new traits
- Partially responsible for diversity of species
- May occur due to translocation (DNA repair mutation)

Evolution

Over the course of many generations of a species, evolution is the change in genetic traits and those expressed. This can be due to mutations in the genes that may be more favorable to survival, or potentially an advantageous combination of inherited genes from an offspring's parents.

Natural Selection
- Proposed by Charles Darwin
- Successful traits of a species increase the likelihood for survival.

Gradualism
- Evolution is slow and gradual.

Punctuated Equilibrium
- Evolution is more abrupt.
- Mutations cause immediate advantages.

Practice Quiz

1. Glycolysis is the catabolism of which type of molecule?

   A. Fatty acids
   B. Amino acids
   C. Monosaccharides
   D. Polysaccharides

2. What combination of characteristics for water is correct?

   A. High specific heat, covalent bonds, cohesive
   B. Low specific heat, covalent bonds, adhesive
   C. High specific heat, ionic bonds, cohesive
   D. Low specific heat, ionic bonds, adhesive

3. Water is an excellent solvent; however, which of the following substances does not mix well with it?

   A. Sugars
   B. Fats
   C. Salts
   D. Enzymes

4. Which of the following processes takes place in the mitochondria of cells?

   A. Photosynthesis
   B. Krebs cycle (citric acid cycle)
   C. Glycolysis
   D. Anaerobic respiration

5. In which phase of mitosis do the spindle fibers attach to the chromosomes, preparing them for separation?

   A. Anaphase
   B. Prophase
   C. Telophase
   D. Prometaphase

6. Testosterone and estrogen are both hormones vital to the sexual function of human males and females. What type of macromolecule are these hormones?

   A. Proteins
   B. Carbohydrates
   C. Lipids
   D. Nucleic acids

7. Which of the following is an example of an enzyme?

   A. Polymerase
   B. Helicase
   C. Amylase
   D. All of the above

8. Bacteria or viruses may infect organisms on a cellular level. Which of the following organelles inside a cell utilizes phagocytosis to eat up the surrounding threats?

   A. Lysosomes
   B. Ribosomes
   C. Vacuoles
   D. Chloroplasts

9. Straight hair in Caucasians is fairly common due to recessive expression of alleles. Which of the following allele combinations would reflect this person's genotype?

   A. *HH*
   B. *Hh*
   C. *hh*
   D. *hH*

10. Which combination of elements and molecules is required for photosynthesis to occur?

    A. Glucose, oxygen, ATP
    B. Oxygen, carbon dioxide, light
    C. Carbon dioxide, water, light
    D. Glucose, protein, oxygen

11. The idea of punctuated equilibrium in reference to evolution has what meaning?

    A. A species evolves slowly over time.
    B. A species does not evolve at all.
    C. A species may experience mutations that cause rapid evolution.
    D. A species evolves via sexual reproduction.

12. Which of the following metabolic reactions manufactures the highest number of ATP for the cell and organism?

    A. Fermentation
    B. Glycolysis
    C. Anaerobic respiration
    D. Citric acid cycle

13. Mitosis yields what type of daughter cells in *Homo sapiens*?

    A. Haploid
    B. Diploid
    C. Triploid
    D. Tetraploid

14. Cystic fibrosis is an autosomal disease that affects the lungs and other organs. When reviewing the genetics of the parents and the potential offspring, where should you focus your attention to detect cystic fibrosis?

    A. Numbered chromosomes
    B. X chromosomes
    C. Y chromosomes
    D. Both X and Y chromosomes

15. If both mother and father are heterozygous for a hair color trait and their child is born with the allele *Bb*, where *B* is brown hair and *b* is blonde hair, how would you interpret the child's allele?

    A. Homozygous recessive and blonde haired
    B. Heterozygous and brown haired
    C. Heterozygous and blonde haired
    D. Homozygous dominant and brown haired

Answer Explanations

1. **C.** Glycolysis is the catabolic reaction breaking down glucose, a monosaccharide, choice C. This process is used to create pyruvate, a molecule in the citric acid cycle (Krebs cycle). None of the other answer choices are involved in glycolysis.

2. **A.** Water has a high specific heat, covalent bonds, and cohesive properties, choice A. None of the other answer choices have the correct combination of characteristics.

3. **B.** Fats/lipids, choice B, are extremely hydrophobic, meaning they are resistant to mixing with water. Think about what happens when you add oil to water; it separates almost immediately. Oil is a type of lipid. Sugar (choice A) mixes easily with water; this is a food source for many organisms. Salts (choice C) also easily dissolve in water; ocean water is a good example. Enzymes (choice D) may also dissolve in water.

4. **B.** Mitochondria are largely responsible for cellular respiration and ATP production in the Krebs cycle (citric acid cycle), choice B. If a cell does not contain mitochondria, it would not be performing this cycle. The only human cells that do not have mitochondria, or a nucleus for that matter, are the red blood cells. Photosynthesis (choice A) is performed in chloroplasts, not in the mitochondria. Glycolysis (choice C) occurs in the cytoplasm of a cell. Anaerobic respiration (choice D) is also performed outside the mitochondria of a cell in the cytoplasm.

5. **D.** During prometaphase, the chromosomes attach to spindle fibers, choice D. During anaphase (choice A), the chromosomes begin separating via the fibers. Telophase (choice C) and cytokinesis will signal the split of the cell. Prophase (choice B) is at the very beginning of mitosis; the chromosomes line up side by side.

6. **C.** Steroid hormones, such as estrogen and testosterone, are four-ring molecules of lipids, choice C, synthesized essentially from cholesterol. Estrogen and testosterone are not proteins (choice A), carbohydrates (choice B), or nucleic acids (choice D).

7. **D.** All molecules that end in "ase" are likely to be enzymes. The correct answer is choice D, all of the above. Polymerase (choice A), helicase (choice B), and amylase (choice C) are all examples of enzymes. Some others include lipase, protease, lactase, and cellulase.

8. **C.** Vacuoles, choice C, play an important role inside a cell. They clean out the cell, removing waste and eating up any foreign entity, if able, by phagocytosis. Lysosomes (choice A) hold enzymes that break down many macromolecules. Ribosomes (choice B) create proteins. Chloroplasts (choice D) are found in plant cells and perform photosynthesis.

9. **C.** Homozygous recessive is displayed in *hh*, choice C. *HH* (choice A) reflects homozygous dominance. *Hh* (choice B) reflects a heterozygous genotype. *hH* (choice D) is not the correct way to write a genotype.

10. **C.** Photosynthesis requires carbon dioxide, water, and light to function, choice C. Glucose (choices A and D) and oxygen (choices A, B, and D) are the byproducts of photosynthesis. ATP (choice A) is not needed for this reaction; nor are proteins (choice D).

11. **C.** Punctuated equilibrium describes a rapid uptick in evolution, potentially from advantageous mutations or genes that are passed down, choice C. Slow evolution over time (choice A) describes gradualism. Most species that do not adapt or evolve (choice B) end up becoming extinct. Sexual reproduction (choice D), while important to evolution and the changing of genes, does not reflect what punctuated equilibrium is.

12. **D.** The Krebs cycle (citric acid cycle) creates, by far, the highest number of ATP during respiration, choice D. Fermentation (choice A), glycolysis (choice B), and anaerobic respiration (choice C) do not create that many ATP. These are not ideal forms of respiration for more complex organisms.

13. **B.** Chromosomes come in pairs in *Homo sapiens* (humans). A pair of chromosomes is called diploid, choice B. The gamete cells of humans are haploid (choice A) because they are singular (not paired). The ploidy options in choices C (triploid) and D (tetraploid) do not exist in humans.

14. **A.** Autosomal diseases are coded in genes that lie on the numbered (nonsex) chromosomes, choice A. X-linked diseases are found on the X chromosomes (choice B). It is very rare that a Y chromosome (choice C) causes disease; the Y chromosome is smaller than the rest and contains far less genetic material in men. Choice D, both X and Y chromosomes, is, therefore, also incorrect.

15. **B.** The allele *Bb* denotes a heterozygous individual. Since the child is heterozygous, the large *B* will dominate over the small *b*. Therefore, the child will have brown hair, making choice B correct. The other answer choices do not reflect the allele *Bb*. The child would only be blonde if the allele were *bb*, a homozygous recessive combination (choice A).

Chapter 6

Chemistry Review

The chemistry section on the HESI A2 contains 25 questions.

Chemistry is, without a doubt, one of the most important aspects of how diseases are managed and diagnosed. Every lab value analyzed, every chemical analysis reviewed, every diagnostic procedure invented—all of these are based in chemistry. For nurses, it is important to understand the basics of chemistry. This allows the delivery of appropriate care and aids in understanding changes in patient status. Chemistry can be a difficult subject for many, especially due to the fact that mathematics is often involved. Subject knowledge is attainable with practice.

Scientific Notation

Being able to write clear and succinct numbers used in science is of the utmost importance. In a hospital setting, even small mistakes may lead to negative consequences. Scientific notation provides an easy-to-read format for conveying large or small numbers. The basis for scientific notation looks like this:

$$C \times 10^n$$

Coefficient/Significand

- Represented above by C
- Cannot be greater than 10 (exponent would increase)

Exponential

- Represented above by 10^n
- The n displays powers of 10 (the exponent).
- May be displayed as E or e
- Examples:
  - 2.3 E5 or 2.3 e5
  - $230,000 = 2.3 \times 10^5$
  - $0.000023 = 2.3 \times 10^{-5}$

HESI Tip: There are some tricks to forming scientific notation. The most common is to move the decimal place and count the number of times it was moved. That number is the exponential. Moving the decimal point to the right results in a positive exponent; moving it to the left yields a negative exponent.

The Metric System

The United States is one of the few countries that does not use the metric system regularly. For nurses, knowledge of the metric system is crucial to working with numbers safely. Administration of medications relies on the metric system, as do many other things. The metric system is used to measure the following:

- Weight (gram)
- Length (meter)
- Volume (liter)

Below are the most common metric units of measurement used by healthcare workers. Notice the metric system functions on multiples of 10. This makes the system very easy to use. Simply move the decimal place to the left or right.

Prefix	Abbreviation	Exponential
kilo	k	10^3
centi	c	10^{-2}
milli	m	10^{-3}
micro	μ	10^{-6}

HESI Tip: Kilogram is commonly used for patient weight. Centimeter is commonly used for patient height. Milligram and microgram are commonly used as dosages for medications.

Multiples of Ten

- 1 g = 1000 mg
- 1 mg = 1000 mcg
- 1 L = 1000 mL

Conversions

- 1 kg = 2.2 lb
- 30 mL = 1 oz
- 1 mL = 1 cc

HESI Tip: Know how to move freely and easily through the metric system—not only for the HESI A2, but also for school and real-world applications. This is a necessary skill to master.

Temperature Scales

Temperature is a piece of chemistry we all experience in the real world. Some temperature scales are used more than others, depending on the intended use and environment. For example, the United States utilizes the Fahrenheit scale. Nearly every other country, however, does not. Celsius, also called centigrade, is the most widely used scale for science, and for the rest of the world.

Fahrenheit

- 98.6° F: Normal body temperature
- 32° F: Water freezes
- Expressed in degrees

Celsius

- 37° C: Normal body temperature
- 0° C: Water freezes
- Expressed in degrees

Kelvin

- 0 K: Absolute zero
- Not expressed in degrees

HESI Tip: Aside from Kelvin, temperature scales use water as a common point of interest and application. It is easy to memorize the benchmarks for water, as they are commonly used in science (e.g., at what temperature does water freeze? boil?).

Atomic Structure

All matter has mass. Matter is made up of atoms that build different types of molecules when bonded together. For example, water is two parts hydrogen and one part oxygen: H_2O. Oxygen and hydrogen are both atoms. Understanding the basic components of molecules will aid in understanding more complex molecules and compounds and their behaviors.

The Atom

- Nucleus
    - Protons (positive charge)
    - Neutrons (no charge)
- Electrons
    - Negative charge
    - Orbit around the nucleus (electron cloud)
    - Form shells (layers of orbit)
    - Valence electron (outermost shell)
- Cation
    - Positively charged atom (ion)
    - Ionic state
- Anion
    - Negatively charged atom (ion)
    - Ionic state

HESI Tip: Each atom has properties that allow it to interact with other atoms. This is most commonly executed by the electrons in the outermost layer of the valence shell, called valence electrons. These electrons are freely available to create a bond and form molecules.

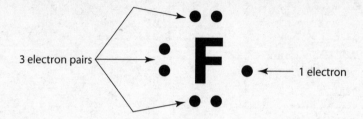

The Periodic Table

- Period/Rows
  - Left to right
- Groups/Columns/Families
  - Top to bottom
- Made up of elements
- Organized by properties and charge of ion
  - Free (open) electrons in outermost shell

The element copper is identified below:

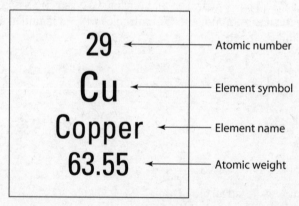

HESI Tip: The elements at the top of the periodic table are those most commonly used and the most important ones for you to learn. Also, be sure to understand the position of noble gases (group 18, far right column) and transition metals (groups 3–12).

PERIODIC TABLE OF THE ELEMENTS

1	2	3	4	5	6	7	8	9	10	11	12	13	14	15	16	17	18
1 **H** 1.008																	2 **He** 4.00
3 **Li** 6.94	4 **Be** 9.01											5 **B** 10.81	6 **C** 12.01	7 **N** 14.01	8 **O** 16.00	9 **F** 19.00	10 **Ne** 20.18
11 **Na** 22.99	12 **Mg** 24.30											13 **Al** 26.98	14 **Si** 28.09	15 **P** 30.97	16 **S** 32.06	17 **Cl** 35.45	18 **Ar** 39.95
19 **K** 39.10	20 **Ca** 40.08	21 **Sc** 44.96	22 **Ti** 47.90	23 **V** 50.94	24 **Cr** 52.00	25 **Mn** 54.94	26 **Fe** 55.85	27 **Co** 58.93	28 **Ni** 58.69	29 **Cu** 63.55	30 **Zn** 65.39	31 **Ga** 69.72	32 **Ge** 72.59	33 **As** 74.92	34 **Se** 78.96	35 **Br** 79.90	36 **Kr** 83.80
37 **Rb** 85.47	38 **Sr** 87.62	39 **Y** 88.91	40 **Zr** 91.22	41 **Nb** 92.91	42 **Mo** 95.94	43 **Tc** (98)	44 **Ru** 101.1	45 **Rh** 102.91	46 **Pd** 106.42	47 **Ag** 107.87	48 **Cd** 112.41	49 **In** 114.82	50 **Sn** 118.71	51 **Sb** 121.75	52 **Te** 127.60	53 **I** 126.91	54 **Xe** 131.29
55 **Cs** 132.91	56 **Ba** 137.33	57 ***La** 138.91	72 **Hf** 178.49	73 **Ta** 180.95	74 **W** 183.85	75 **Re** 186.21	76 **Os** 190.2	77 **Ir** 192.2	78 **Pt** 195.08	79 **Au** 196.97	80 **Hg** 200.59	81 **Tl** 204.38	82 **Pb** 207.2	83 **Bi** 208.98	84 **Po** (209)	85 **At** (210)	86 **Rn** (222)
87 **Fr** (223)	88 **Ra** 226.02	89 **†Ac** 227.03	104 **Rf** (261)	105 **Db** (262)	106 **Sg** (266)	107 **Bh** (264)	108 **Hs** (277)	109 **Mt** (268)	110 **Ds** (271)	111 **Rg** (272)							

*Lanthanide Series

58 **Ce** 140.12	59 **Pr** 140.91	60 **Nd** 144.24	61 **Pm** (145)	62 **Sm** 150.4	63 **Eu** 151.97	64 **Gd** 157.25	65 **Tb** 158.93	66 **Dy** 162.50	67 **Ho** 164.93	68 **Er** 167.26	69 **Tm** 168.93	70 **Yb** 173.04	71 **Lu** 174.97
90 **Tn** 232.04	91 **Pa** 231.04	92 **U** 238.03	93 **Np** (237)	94 **Pu** (244)	95 **Am** (243)	96 **Cm** (247)	97 **Bk** (247)	98 **Cf** (251)	99 **Es** (252)	100 **Fm** (257)	101 **Md** (258)	102 **No** (259)	103 **Lr** (262)

†Actinide Series

Atomic Matter

- Mass is very small in size.
- Atomic mass is measured in moles.
- Mass is mostly protons plus neutrons.
- Example: $2 H_2 + O_2 = H_2O$
  - 2 moles of hydrogen + 1 mole of oxygen
- Mass is neither created nor destroyed (stoichiometry).
- Isotopes
  - Alternate forms of atoms
  - Proton and electron number stays same
  - Neutron number changes
  - Example: radioactive isotopes (carbon dating, PET scans, cancer treatments)

States of Matter

Matter can exist in a variety of forms. The most common difference between forms is the density of the matter and atoms. Water is frequently referred to when referencing states of matter because it can be a solid, liquid, or gas. It is also one of the few molecules that is less dense in solid form than in liquid form—ice floats in liquid water.

Solids

- Tightly packed atoms
- Generally a grid format
- No free movement; atoms vibrate

Liquids

- Loosely held atoms
- Matter is "melted."

Gases

- Distantly spread atoms
- Diffuses (moves around) faster than other states of matter
- Matter is vaporized.

Chemical Bonding

Unstable atoms (ions) are in a constant state of movement and seek out other atoms to bond with or become stable with. Every molecule or compound is bonded in some form.

Covalent Bonds

- Sharing of electrons between atoms
  - Single bond: One electron shared
  - Double bond: Two electrons shared
- Strongest type of bond
- Equal sharing of electrons (nonpolar)
- Unequal sharing of electrons (polar)

Ionic Bonds

- Transfer of electrons between atoms

Polar Bonds

- Unequal sharing of electrons between atoms
- One end of the molecule is stronger (more negatively charged, more electrons).
- Occurs in covalent bonding

Intermolecular Forces

- Weaker than other bonds
- Hydrogen bonds: Affinity by hydrogen atoms
- Dipole-dipole
  - Alignment of polar ends of a molecule
- Dispersion forces
  - Temporary polar atoms
  - Very weak attraction

HESI Tip: Understanding the specifics on how atoms form molecules is commonly taught in organic chemistry. This is not an in-depth topic on the HESI A2. A general understanding is required here.

Chemical Equations

When reviewing chemical equations, note that half of an atom does not exist, nor does half of a molecule. Equations must be balanced to account for the fact that matter is neither created nor destroyed (law of conservation). Each side of the equation must equal the same moles of each element. Sometimes it is necessary to balance an equation by multiplying each coefficient by a number, such as 2 or 3.

Example:

$$NaHCO_3 + HC_2H_3O_2 \rightarrow NaC_2H_3O_2 + H_2O + CO_2$$

The above chemical equation is a tried-and-true "volcano" experiment many children perform out of curiosity and the desired "wow" factor. Below is simplified verbiage for better understanding.

baking soda + vinegar $\rightarrow$ sodium acetate + water + carbon dioxide

HESI Tip: For the record, it is the carbon dioxide that gives this volcano experiment that bubbling reaction we love so much!

Reactants

- Input elements and/or molecules on the left
- Baking soda and vinegar (above example)

Products

- Output elements and/or molecules on the right
- Sodium acetate, water, and carbon dioxide (above example)

Reaction Properties

- Equilibrium: A point of reaction stability
- Reversibility: Reactants may make products, products may make reactants
- Increasing the rate (speed) of reaction
  - Increase temperature.
  - Increase surface area.
  - Utilize a catalyst (reusable).
  - Increase concentration of reactants.

HESI Tip: Changes in equilibrium cause a system to compensate. In chemistry this is called Le Chatelier's principle. In biology, the concept is called hemostasis.

Solutions

There are many types of solutions. For a mixture to be considered a solution it must be homogeneous (the same) and contain two or more substances mixed together. The particles must be spread out evenly across the mixture.

Here are a few examples of homogeneous solutions:

- Compound
- Alloy
- Emulsion

HESI Tip: The opposite of a homogeneous solution is a heterogeneous solution. The particles in a heterogeneous solution clump together and do not spread out easily, such as in a suspension.

Solution Terminology

- Solute: Dissolves in solvent
- Solvent: Absorbs solute
- Miscible: Dissolvable

- Immiscible: Not dissolvable
- Aqueous: Water solvent

Concentration

- Percent: Common percentage by mass or volume

HESI Tip: In health care, most concentrations are expressed as mg per mL. For example, many IV bags, such as antibiotics, are ordered as mg per mL.

- Molarity: Moles of solute per liter (solution)
- Dilute: Less solute in solution
- Concentrated: More solute in solution

HESI Tip: Avogadro's number is 6.02×10^{23}. This number reflects the number of units in one mole of any substance, which is defined as the substance's molecular weight in grams.

Chemical Reactions

How an atom reacts with another atom is chemical. How a molecule is created or destroyed is also chemical. There are different types of reactions that occur, but all matter reacts in this manner. Take the human body, for example—the breakdown of food by catalysts called enzymes is accomplished by a series of chemical reactions that begins in the mouth with saliva. Below are the five most common types of chemical reactions: synthesis/combination, decomposition, combustion, single replacement, and double replacement.

HESI Tip: Catalysts speed up a reaction. Oftentimes without catalysts or enzymes, in the biological sense, certain reactions would take far too long to be beneficial to an organism. A reaction can also be sped up by increasing the temperature or increasing the surface area.

Synthesis/Combination

- Elements combine to create a product.
- $A + B \rightarrow C$
- $O_2 + 2H_2 \rightarrow 2\,H_2O$

Decomposition

- Breakdown of compounds to smaller parts
- $C \rightarrow A + B$
- $2\,H_2O \rightarrow 2\,H_2 + O_2$

Combustion

- Exothermic: Releases energy (heat, light)
- Fuel (hydrocarbons: fuel or gas) + oxygen $\rightarrow CO_2 + H_2O$
- Example: Car engine

Single Replacement

- Movement of one reactant by another
- Copper placed in silver nitrate
  - $2 \, AgNO_3 + Cu \rightarrow Cu \, (NO_3)_2 + 2 \, Ag$
  - Copper is more reactive than silver (copper displaces).

Double Replacement

- Exchange of two compounds (ionic)
- Positive and negative ions swap
- $AC + BD \rightarrow AD + BC$
- $AgNO_3 + NaCl \rightarrow AgCl + NaNO_3$

Stoichiometry

The law of conservation of mass states that matter can neither be created nor destroyed. This must be taken into account when analyzing chemical equations. A certain amount of reactants will always be needed to form a certain amount of products. The equation must be balanced. Empirical equations allow this to happen.

Dimensional Analysis

- Used to calculate and balance equations

Oxidation and Reduction

Often called redox, these reactions occur when an electron is either lost or gained. An oxidized element will lose electrons; the reduced element gains electrons. Electrons, by nature, are negatively charged particles. By movement of electrons, the overall charge within a reaction changes. These reactions may also involve the movement of oxygen or hydrogen.

Oxidation Numbers

- The oxidation number is the charge of the ion.
  - Example: NaCl (table salt), a stable compound with charge 0: Na^+Cl^-
    $Na^+ = +1$
    $Cl^- = -1$

Finding the Oxidation Number

- Hydrogen oxidation number = +1
- Oxygen oxidation number = −2
- Chlorine oxidation number = −1

Use the above information to formulate the oxidation number for elements in compounds. Coefficients in chemical equations do not matter for oxidation numbers. Every molecule is stable with a charge of 0. Keep that in mind. For example, let's look at the molecule of methane:

$$CH_4$$

This molecule is one part carbon and four parts hydrogen. Hydrogen has an oxidation number of +1. There are four hydrogens in CH_4, so $(+1) \times 4 = +4$. Since all oxidation numbers must add up to zero, carbon must have an oxidation number of –4: $(+4) + (-4) = 0$.

HESI Tip: There are exceptions to the rules above in advanced chemistry; for the HESI A2, use the above simplified rules.

Acids and Bases

The pH Scale

- 0 to 7: Acidotic (acid)
- 7: pH neutral (water)
- 7–14: Alkalotic (base)
- pH indicator color changes:
  - Acids: Indicator shows change from green toward red
  - Bases: Indicator shows change from green toward purple

HESI Tip: The letters "pH" stand for "potential of hydrogen." Most people never see it written out like that and are only familiar with the abbreviated term "pH." Knowing that hydrogen is the key player in overall acidity and alkalinity helps you grasp the concept.

Acids

- Donate hydrogens or protons
- Less acidic when bases added
- Change blue litmus red
- Dissolve certain metals
- Sour taste

Bases

- Accept hydrogens or protons
- Neutralize acids
- Change red litmus to blue
- Conduct electricity
- Commonly have hydroxide group (OH)
- Alkaline

HESI Tip: When an acid or base is fairly close to a pH of 7, it is typically called "weak." These weak acids and bases do not completely donate their protons (weak acids) or ionize entirely (weak bases). Strong acids and bases lie toward the ends of the spectrum.

HESI Tip: When a molecule acts as both an acid and a base, it is called amphoteric. Water is a common molecule that acts in this manner.

Nuclear Chemistry

What happens in the nucleus of an atom and how the nucleus finds stability is the focus of nuclear chemistry. When a nucleus is unstable, it may release energy in the form of radiation. In this sense, the atom is described as radioactive.

Alpha Radiation

- Very large particles
- Stopped easily with paper

Beta Radiation

- Negative or positive charge
- Stopped by thin aluminum

Gamma Radiation

- Electromagnetic radiation
- X-ray–type radiation
- Very damaging (cancer causing)
- Lead shield used for protection

Radioactive Isotopes

- Isotopes
  - Same proton number, different neutron number
  - Stable
  - Unstable (radioactive)
- Written in two manners:
  - Carbon-14
  - 14C

HESI Tip: The above example of carbon, carbon-14, is used in the real world. It allows us to find out how old something is through identification of the radioisotope decay. This is commonly referred to as carbon dating.

- Unstable isotopes
  - Half-life: Amount of time for half to decay or become stable
  - Radioactive

Biochemistry

Biochemistry largely deals with the macromolecules utilized by living organisms. The metabolism of these macromolecules, how they are built and utilized, is also learned in biochemistry. Carbohydrates, lipids, proteins, and nucleic acids are the hallmark macromolecules.

These topics were discussed in Chapter 5, "Biology Review." Refer to that chapter for a refresher on macromolecules, focusing on the following for the purposes of biochemistry:

1. Study the atoms and bonds of each macromolecule.
   a. What does the molecule look like?
2. How do these macromolecules interact with organisms?

For reference, each molecular structure and examples are provided below, displaying what makes up these chemical compounds. However, the biological applications are found in the biology chapter on pp. 32–34.

Carbohydrates

- Monosaccharides (simple carbohydrate)
  - Glucose ($C_6H_{12}O_6$)
  - 1:2:1 ratio of carbon to hydrogen to oxygen
- Oligosaccharides
  - Three to six monosaccharides connected
- Polysaccharides (complex sugars)
  - Starches (glycogen)
  - Cellulose
- Contain pentoses (5-carbon chain)
- Liver/kidneys can create glucose (gluconeogenesis).
- Utilized in Krebs cycle (ATP production)
  - Glycolysis: Breakdown of glucose to pyruvate

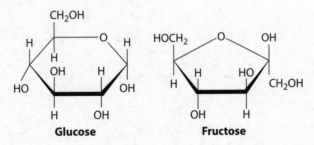

Glucose   Fructose

Proteins

- Made up of amino acids
- Contain peptide bonds
  - Dipeptide: Two amino acids
  - Polypeptide: Many amino acids
- Many amino acids exist (20 important to humans).
- Examples:
  - Albumin, a crucial protein in blood
  - Enzymes, a catalyst to speed up reactions

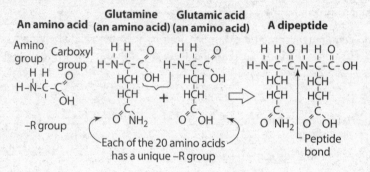

Lipids

- Made up of fatty acids (long hydrocarbon chain) and glycerol
- Saturated fatty acid (no double bond)
- Unsaturated fatty acid (contains a double bond)
  - Appears bent
  - Healthier in food than saturated fatty acids
- Examples:
  - Oils
  - Cholesterol triglycerides

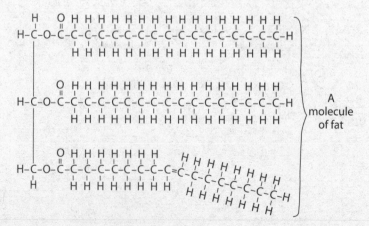

Nucleic Acids

- Very large particles
  - Sugar-phosphate groups repeat.
- Deoxyribonucleic acid (DNA): Two-strand double helix
- Ribonucleic acid (RNA): One-strand ribose chain
  - Uracil replaces thymine
- Examples:
  - DNA and RNA

In chemistry, when compounds contain carbon, the term "organic chemistry" is generally used. All of the macromolecules described above could be called organic. The human body is organic. All living things are organic.

Thermodynamics

The topic of thermodynamics is discussed more in Chapter 8, "Physics Review," since it is more of a segment in that study. For chemistry, however, there is a special application of thermodynamics as it relates to chemical reactions; specifically, heat and work. Thermodynamics can also be discussed in relation to changes between phases of matter, such as liquid to gas.

Energy

- The amount of energy from a chemical reaction
- Example: Calories in food
- Called "internal energy"

Entropy

- Energy potential not in use

Enthalpy

- Internal energy plus pressure and volume
- May determine release of heat by reactions
- May change between phase changes of matter

Gibbs Free Energy

- Available energy
- Decreases as systems find equilibrium

Practice Quiz

1. Calculate the mass (in grams) of four moles of potassium chloride (KCl). Reference the periodic table (p. 53).

    A. 39.10
    B. 74.55
    C. 149.10
    D. 298.20

2. What is the name of the vertical columns on the periodic table?

    A. Families
    B. Periods
    C. Blocks
    D. Lines

3. When running a motor vehicle, hydrocarbons are often burned to create energy. Carbon dioxide is released. What type of reaction is this?

    A. Single replacement
    B. Synthesis
    C. Decomposition
    D. Combustion

4. What is the name of the molecular compound SO_3?

    A. Sulfur trioxide
    B. Sulfur dioxide
    C. Sodium dioxide
    D. Sodium chloride

5. What does the atomic number explain?

    A. The number of protons plus neutrons
    B. The number of protons
    C. The number of valence electrons
    D. The total weight of the atom

6. What is the best description of gluconeogenesis?

    A. The creation of glucose by the liver or kidneys
    B. The creation of proteins from amino acids
    C. The creation of cholesterol from food
    D. The creation of DNA

7. Many of the medications given in a hospital have a dosage that is based off of weight. If a patient weighs 220 pounds, what is the patient's weight in kilograms?

   A. 55 kg
   B. 100 kg
   C. 110 kg
   D. 440 kg

8. Helium is considered a noble gas of the periodic table group 18 (also called group VIIIA). Noble gases very rarely undergo chemical reactions because of what key point?

   A. These elements have no charge.
   B. These elements have large mass.
   C. These elements have no free electrons in the outer shell.
   D. These elements are already bonded to other elements.

9. Reactants may make products and products may make reactants. What is the name of the ability for chemical reactions to work both ways?

   A. Equilibrium
   B. Reversibility
   C. Catalyst-driven reactions
   D. Compensation

10. The law of conservation of mass says that matter can neither be created nor destroyed. What is the name for this principle in chemistry when balancing equations of reactants and products?

    A. Transference
    B. Equilibrium
    C. Stoichiometry
    D. Single replacement

11. Polar bonds between atoms are best described by what?

    A. Equal sharing of electrons resulting in polar ends
    B. Unequal sharing of electrons resulting in one stronger polar end
    C. The polarity of each molecule end changes.
    D. Electrons are constantly moving and polarity cannot be known.

12. What type of radiation is known to cause the most harm (cancer) in humans?

    A. Gamma radiation
    B. Alpha radiation
    C. Beta radiation
    D. All radiation can cause cancer.

13. Which of the following descriptions of DNA and RNA is true?

    A. Are most commonly found outside the nucleus
    B. Are mostly made up of glycerol and fatty acids
    C. Are simple molecules
    D. Are made up of nucleotides that contain sugar

14. An atom with a negative charge is called a(n)

    A. Isotope
    B. Electron
    C. Anion
    D. Cation

15. Which of the following most accurately describes the valence electrons of an atom?

    A. The electrons available for ionic bonding
    B. The electrons available for covalent bonding
    C. The electrons available for any atomic bonding
    D. The outermost electrons that create polar bonds

Answer Explanations

1. **D.** To calculate the mass of any molecule, add up the atomic mass of each individual element. The atomic mass of potassium is 39.10. The atomic mass of chlorine is 35.45. Therefore, the total mass of one mole of potassium chloride is 74.55. Multiply 74.55 times 4 to achieve the total mass of four moles of KCl: $74.55 \times 4 = 298.20$, choice D.

2. **A.** The vertical columns on the periodic table are called groups or families, choice A. Periods (choice B) are the horizontal rows. Neither blocks (choice C) nor lines (choice D) reflect any term for the table.

3. **D.** Combustion, choice D, is a reaction where the reactants are hydrocarbons such as CH4 (methane) and oxygen. The products of this reaction are carbon dioxide and water. This is the essential reaction that all motor vehicles run on. A single replacement reaction (choice A) has one element swapping or changing out with another. A synthesis reaction (choice B) is about the creation of a single molecule (product) with two or more reactants. A decomposition reaction (choice C) is the opposite of a synthesis reaction. It breaks down a larger reactant into smaller separate products.

4. **A.** Use the periodic table provided (see p. 53) to find the element in a given molecule. S is the element symbol for sulfur. The harder part can be to put together the full name of a molecule. In this case, oxygen (O) takes on the name "oxide" when combined with another element. There are three atoms of oxygen to give the prefix "tri." Therefore, SO_3 is sodium trioxide, choice A.

5. **B.** The atomic number is the number of protons found in the nucleus of an atom, choice B. In a neutral atom, the number of electrons is equal to the number of protons. Aside from isotopes, all atoms have a neutral, zero balance; the protons and electrons balance each other out. The number of protons plus neutrons (choice A) is the atomic mass. The number of valence electrons (choice C) is not reflected by the atomic number. The total weight of the atom (choice D) could also be called the atomic mass; this is reflected by adding up the protons and neutrons (same as choice A).

6. **A.** Gluconeogenesis is one of the processes the body goes through when it needs to create glucose (sugar), choice A. It does this by breaking down other forms of energy such as fat or protein. Proteins are made from amino acids by RNA in a process called transcription (choice B). The creation of DNA (choice D) is called replication. Cholesterol is built by the process synthesis (choice C); broken-down food products are built back into this specialized lipid steroid, also called a sterol.

7. **B.** The conversion 2.2 kg = 1 lb is used for this question. Therefore, $220 \text{ lb} \div 2.2 = 100 \text{ kg}$, choice B.

8. **C.** The noble gases, positioned in the far-right column on the periodic table, have no available electrons to interact with other elements, choice C. The outer valence shell is completely full. Because the valence shell is full, these atoms very rarely bond to or react with other elements (choice D). It is true that these elements typically have no charge (choice A); however, that is not why they do not interact with other elements. The noble gases have a wide range of atomic masses, and their mass has nothing to do with why they typically do not interact with other elements (choice B).

9. **B.** The word "reverse" in English typically means to move backward or change direction. In chemistry, the meaning is quite similar. Reversibility is a chemical reaction's ability to turn around and go back the way it came, choice B. Equilibrium (choice A) means that a chemical reaction has reached the point where reactants and products have a concentration that no longer causes the reaction to occur. Catalyst-driven reactions (choice C) imply the use of a catalyst or, in biology, an enzyme. This speeds up the reaction. Compensation (choice D) is the tendency of a system to rebound in the other direction to find an equilibrium point when a change is made.

10. **C.** The basic principle of stoichiometry is that equations must be balanced. A reactant to an equation cannot outweigh the products; they must be equal. The same principle is the basis for the law of conservation of mass: Matter can neither be destroyed nor created. Stoichiometry, choice C, is correct. Transference (choice A) is not a term used in chemistry. Equilibrium (choice B) describes the point where a chemical reaction no longer occurs due to equal concentrations. Single replacement (choice D) is a term for a type of chemical reaction, not this principle.

11. **B.** Polarity is the differences in electrical charge of a molecule. One end of the molecule has a positive charge; the other end, a negative charge. This polarity creates bonds or affinity between certain ends of molecules. A good example is H_2O or water. There is an unequal sharing of the electrons in these types of molecules, choice B.

12. **A.** Gamma radiation, choice A, causes cancer in humans. Not all types of radiation cause cancer (choice D). Alpha radiation (choice B), for example, does not penetrate the skin. Beta radiation (choice C) has been known to cause some damage to the human body and in some cases is used for treatment, such as radiation to kill cancer cells. Beta radiation, however, is not as damaging as gamma radiation, which requires extensive shielding to protect humans that are exposed to it.

13. **D.** DNA and RNA are constructed by using nucleotides. These nucleotides contain a 5-carbon chain of sugar, a phosphate group, and a base. Therefore, choice D is correct. DNA and RNA are most commonly found inside the nucleus, not outside (choice A). They often leave the nucleus to aid in replication and creation of proteins, but the majority of their time is spent inside the nucleus. As described above, DNA and RNA contain nucleotides; these are not made up of glycerol or fatty acids (choice B). DNA and RNA are complex, not simple, molecules (choice C). The construction and replication of both require many processes.

14. **C.** Anions are negatively charged particles, choice C. Cations (choice D) are positively charged particles. An electron (choice B) is a component of an atom, not the atom itself. An isotope (choice A) does not change the charge, but rather the number of neutrons and mass.

15. **C.** The valence electrons or valence shell is the available electrons for any atomic bonding, choice C. This type of bonding varies, depending on the element; it could be ionic (choice A) or covalent (choice B). The number of valence electrons depends on the atom itself. For example, carbon has four valence electrons available for bonding. Polar bonds (choice D) describe the polarity of a molecule being created, not the atom itself.

Chapter 7

Anatomy and Physiology Review

The anatomy and physiology section on the HESI A2 contains 25 questions.

Arguably the most important pieces of information to understand, anatomy and physiology are the building blocks of scientific knowledge leading into nursing school. It is of utmost importance to grasp medical terminology in relation to anatomy and physiology. As you progress through nursing school and your career, it is impossible to advance to more difficult topics without mastering the basics. How could anyone discuss or treat a liver problem without even knowing where the liver is inside the body?

It is also recommended that even if you do not need to take the biology section on your HESI A2, study it in this book to grasp the basics. Pay particular attention to cellular biology, mitosis/meiosis, and macromolecules (carbs, fats, proteins, nucleic acids). Our body is entirely made up of cells, which are the building blocks of all living things. The anatomy and physiology of every organ, every body mechanism, and every action are grounded by cells and what they create and do.

General Terminology

Much of medical terminology is based in Latin, so there are common themes across the board. It would be wise to master terminology now before advancing into more difficult topics. It cannot be overstated how much easier your studies become when terminology is understood. This can be difficult depending on one's native language. Many languages are based in Latin, but many are not. Below is an introduction to terminology.

Homeostasis
- Balance within normal limits of the body
- Negative feedback
  - Abnormal conditions trigger a response to correct
    - Examples: Insulin release, water regulation
- Positive feedback
  - Condition triggers an increase in process
    - Examples: Blood clotting, labor
  - Uncommon

Terminology Basics
- Apex region
  - Central area
  - Head, neck, and trunk (torso)
- Appendicular region
  - Peripheral area
  - Appendages (arms and legs)

- Body planes/sections:

Frontal plane (coronal)	Transverse plane (horizontal)	Sagittal plane
■ Divides body/organ into anterior and posterior portions	■ Divides body/organ into superior and inferior portions	■ Divides body/organ into right and left portions ■ Midsagittal (equal portions) ■ Parasagittal (unequal portions)

- Body cavities (contain organs):

Ventral cavity	Dorsal cavity
■ Thoracic cavity (lungs and heart) ○ Mediastinum (heart) ■ Abdominopelvic cavity	■ Cranial cavity (brain) ■ Vertebral cavity (spinal cord)

HESI Tip: Ventral means the front of the body. Dorsal means the back side. An easy way to remember this is to think of a dorsal fin of a dolphin; it is on the back of the animal.

- Directional terminology:

Term	Definition
Superior	Above an area
Inferior	Below an area
Ventral/anterior	Toward front of the body
Dorsal/posterior	Toward back of the body
Medial	Midline of the body
Lateral	Sides of the body
Proximal	Toward point of limb attachment
Distal	Away from point of limb attachment
Superficial	Toward surface of the body
Deep	Toward inside of the body

Tissues

The study of tissues and cells is referred to as histology. With the help of a microscope, it is possible to analyze tissues and individual cells. There are hundreds of types of cells within the human body; understanding each type of cell forms the basis for many specialties within medicine and nursing.

When cells come together to form a similar purpose, they make tissues. When tissues come together to form a similar purpose, they make organs. Take cardiac muscle tissue, for example; each individual cardiac muscle cell (myocardiocyte) has the power to individually beat. With the combined mass of many myocardiocytes, the organ (heart) works to pump blood throughout the body.

Epithelial Tissue

- Lining of areas on and inside the body
- Types of epithelium:

Simple epithelium: One layer	Stratified epithelium: Multiple layers
Pseudostratified epithelium: One layer (varying sizes)	Transitional epithelium: Stretches

- Glandular epithelium
  - Endocrine glands: Secrete hormones into bloodstream (thyroxine, insulin, etc.)
  - Exocrine glands: Secrete into tubes or ducts (saliva, sebum, etc.)

HESI Tip: Certain types of epithelial cells contain microvilli. These microvilli greatly increase the surface area, which increases the amount of a substance that can be absorbed. A good example is the small intestine. Certain diseases exist when people have issues with absorption (celiac disease, etc.).

Connective Tissue

- Crucial in maintaining structure (matrix)
  - Made of collagen and reticular and elastic fibers
- Types of connective tissue:

Loose connective	Dense connective	Cartilage
- Adipose (fat)	- Regular	- Fibrocartilage
- Reticular	- Irregular	- Hyaline
- Areolar		- Elastic
Bone (osseous)	**Blood and lymph (vascular)**	
- Compact	- Liquid matrix	
- Spongy		

- Types of membranes (connective and epithelial tissues):

Serous	Mucous
- Line internal organs	- Line body cavities
- Contain serous fluid (clear lubricant)	- Examples: Mouth, nose, urethra
- Examples: Pleural cavity, pericardium	
Synovial	**Cutaneous**
- Bone joints	- Skin

Nervous Tissue

- Types of nervous tissue:

Neurons	Glial
- Foundation of nervous system	- Support for neurons
	- Schwann cells (neurolemmocytes)
	o Form myelin sheath

Muscle Tissue

- Types of muscle tissue:

Skeletal muscle	Cardiac muscle	Smooth muscle
- Voluntary	- Involuntary	- Involuntary
- Striated	- Striated	- Not striated
- Multicellular (ATP production)	- Heart muscle	- Vessels, digestive tract

HESI Tip: When talking about muscle, the word "voluntary" refers to being able to control the movement. Skeletal muscle is considered voluntary because the decision to move an arm or walk down a sidewalk is a conscious thought. One cannot tell the heart to beat faster or constrict a blood vessel; these are involuntary movements.

The Integumentary System

The skin is the largest organ of the human body. With vast responsibilities in keeping the human body functioning, the integumentary system comes to the forefront when it is malfunctioning. From burns to rashes, vitiligo to wounds, the range of severity and symptoms of the skin are vast and often serve as markers for underlying internal disease.

Epidermis

- Anatomy
  - Multiple layers of squamous cells
    - 4 layers for normal skin
    - 5 layers for thick skin (palms and soles):

Stratum corneum	Stratum lucidum	Stratum granulosum
■ Dead keratinized cells ■ Top layer	■ Thick skin (palms of hands and soles of feet) ■ Not present in other skin	■ Keratin forms by keratohyalin granules
Stratum spinosum	Stratum germinativum	
	■ Basal layer ■ Single layer of cells ■ Active mitosis	

  - Keratin (protein in hair, skin, nails)
    - Protects skin from damage, water, invading pathogens, etc.
  - Melanin (pigmentation)
  - Merkel disc (sensory input)
- Physiology
  - First line of defense (pathogens and damage)
  - Produces vitamin D
    - Synthesizes upon sunlight (UV)
    - Aids in bone strength
  - Sensation
    - Nociceptors (pressure, pain, etc.)
  - Temperature regulation
    - Sweating duct (sudoriferous glands)

Dermis

- Anatomy
  - o Connective tissues (collagen, reticular, and elastic)
  - o Two layers:

Papillary layer	Reticular layer
■ Outer layer	■ Thick layer
■ Sebaceous gland (sebum - oil)	■ Majority of dermis
■ Dermal papillae	■ Hair follicles
■ Pushes into epidermis	■ Blood vessels
■ Fingerprints	■ Nerve endings

- Physiology
  - o Elasticity (movement)
  - o Protection from collagen (damage or trauma)
  - o Delivers nutrients to skin (blood vessels)
  - o Sensation of pain, temperature, pressure, etc.

Hypodermis

- Anatomy
  - o Subcutaneous tissue
  - o Not a part of the skin
  - o Adipose tissue (fat)
- Physiology
  - o Anchors skin to lower structures
  - o Fat provides insulation.
  - o Prevents damage to underlying structures (organs, muscles, and bones)
  - o Storage of energy in fat

Accessory Organs

- Hair follicles
  - o Arrector pili muscle (goose bumps)
  - o Temperature regulation
- Sudoriferous (sweat) glands
  - o Temperature regulation, milk production, cerumen (earwax), and apocrine (sex, puberty)
- Nails
- Sebaceous (oil) glands
  - o Release sebum
  - o Protect skin from drying out
  - o Prevent bacterial proliferation

HESI Tip: Many skin diseases are linked to problems within the layers of the skin. For example, a sebaceous gland that becomes occluded and infected with bacteria is the common cause of acne.

The Skeletal System

While being able to recite the roughly 206 bones in the human body is impressive, the skeletal system and the understanding of this body system is much more important than simple recitation. A common misconception of the skeletal system is that it is not alive. This could not be further from the truth. The skeletal system is constantly remodeling itself and adapting to current stresses and demands.

The skeletal system is responsible for structure and support, as well as nutrient storage and delivery. This section will discuss the complexities of this important body system.

Skeletal System Components

Bone	Cartilage	Tendons
■ Connective tissue mineralized with calcium phosphate and collagen ■ Strong structural component	■ Flexible connective tissue ■ Protects bone (lubricates) ■ Articular joints ■ Chondrocytes (build cartilage)	■ Strong connective tissue of collagen ■ Connect muscle to bone
Ligaments	**Joints**	
■ Strong connective tissue of collagen ■ Connect bone to bone	■ Articular connections of the skeletal system ■ Articulating bones ■ Allow for movement and bending ■ Synovial joints (contain synovial fluid)	

Bone Terminology

Compact bone	Spongy bone
■ Contains osteon units ■ Hard outer shell of many bones ■ Osteon: See "Bone Structure" graphic on the next page for in-depth analysis of osteon.	■ Loose interior bone, not as strong ■ Lattice or porous network (trabeculae) ■ Contains red bone marrow (red blood cell production - hematopoiesis)
Long bone	**Flat bone**
■ Epiphysis: Ends of the bone responsible for growth in childhood ■ Epiphyseal plate: Area of bone growth ■ Epiphyseal line: Hardened old cartilage from childhood growth ■ Yellow marrow: Made of adipose tissue and stem cells ■ Examples: Femur, tibia, humerus	■ Thin bone ■ Examples: Cranium (sutural), ribs
Irregular bone	**Bone membrane**
■ No standard shape ■ Examples: Vertebrae, facial bones	■ Periosteum: Outside membrane covering compact bone ■ Endosteum: Interior membrane of marrow
Osseous tissue and osteons	
■ Osteoblasts: Bone-building cells ■ Osteoclasts: Bone-destroying cells ■ Osteocytes: Mature bone cells ■ Ossification: Process of building compact bone (hyaline cartilage turns to bone)	

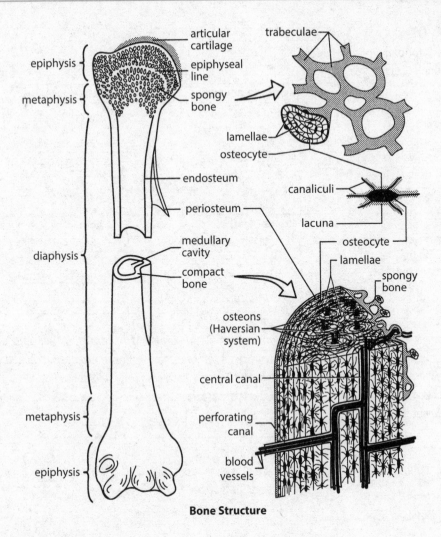

Bone Structure

The Human Skeleton

The section below goes into more depth on the individual bones of the skeletal system. For the purpose of the HESI A2, this review is entry-level in nature. A full overview of the skeletal system will follow in nursing school when discussing the musculoskeletal system as a whole, along with the many diseases and problems that can occur in the system. Entry-level knowledge will provide the ability to say "the femur is a long bone in the thigh; a part of the appendicular skeleton."

Axial Skeleton

- Central components of the system
- Major bone segments:

Thorax	Vertebral column	Facial bones
<ul><li>Sternum (manubrium, body, and xiphoid process)</li><li>Ribs (12 pairs, 2 floating rib pairs)</li><li>Protects lungs and heart</li><li>Intercostal spaces (space between ribs)</li></ul>	<ul><li>Cervical (7), thoracic (12), and lumbar (5) vertebrae</li><li>Sacrum</li><li>Coccyx (tailbone)</li><li>Protects spinal cord</li><li>See vertebrae graphic on the next page for in-depth bone analysis.</li></ul>	<ul><li>Mandible (lower jaw)</li><li>Maxilla (upper jaw)</li><li>Zygomatic (cheek)</li><li>Sinuses (nasal)</li></ul>
Cranium	**Ossicles (ear)**	**Hyoid**
<ul><li>Frontal, parietal, temporal, sphenoid, ethmoid, and occipital</li><li>Protects the brain</li><li>Fontanels (soft membrane) until roughly age 2</li></ul>	<ul><li>Stapes, incus, and malleus</li><li>Transmit sound to cochlea</li><li>Stapes: Smallest bone in the body</li></ul>	<ul><li>Small bone in the neck</li><li>Not connected to other bones</li><li>Supports tongue</li></ul>

HESI Tip: Learning terminology may seem tedious at times, and it certainly is, but it will help down the line. For example, a laminectomy is a surgery that relieves pressure off of nerves in the spine causing pain. If you know the meaning of the word "lamina" you can decipher the meaning of "laminectomy." The lamina is a layer of bony spinal canal that protects the nerves of the spinal cord. Everything in knowledge is connected, especially when advancing to more difficult topics.

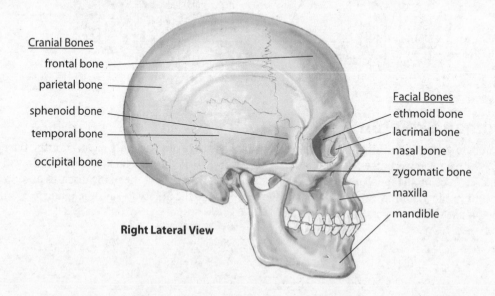

Cranial Bones
- frontal bone
- parietal bone
- sphenoid bone
- temporal bone
- occipital bone

Facial Bones
- ethmoid bone
- lacrimal bone
- nasal bone
- zygomatic bone
- maxilla
- mandible

Right Lateral View

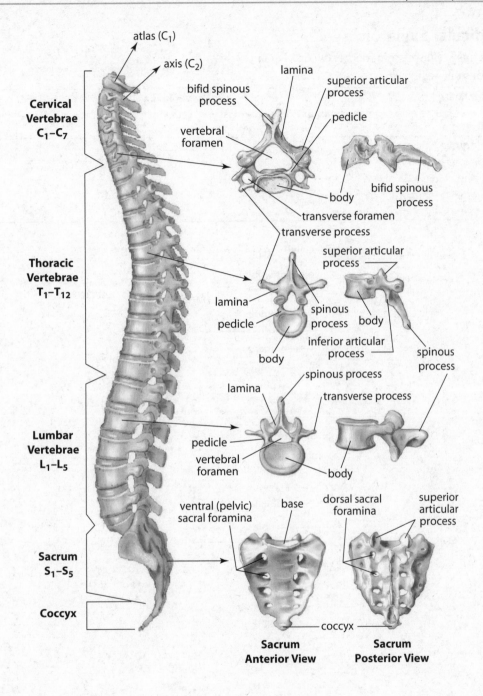

atlas (C₁)

axis (C₂)

Cervical Vertebrae C₁–C₇

lamina

bifid spinous process

superior articular process

pedicle

vertebral foramen

bifid spinous process

body

transverse foramen

transverse process

Thoracic Vertebrae T₁–T₁₂

superior articular process

lamina

spinous process

pedicle

body

body

inferior articular process

spinous process

lamina

spinous process

transverse process

Lumbar Vertebrae L₁–L₅

pedicle

vertebral foramen

body

spinous process

ventral (pelvic) sacral foramina

base

dorsal sacral foramina

superior articular process

Sacrum S₁–S₅

Coccyx

coccyx

Sacrum Anterior View

Sacrum Posterior View

Appendicular Skeleton

- Appendage (limbs) components of the system
- Major bone segments:

Upper limbs	Lower limbs
▪ Humerus, ulna, radius, carpals, metacarpals, and phalanges	▪ Femur, patella, tibia, fibula, tarsals, metatarsals, and phalanges
Pelvic girdle	**Pectoral girdle**
▪ Ilium, ischium, and pubis ▪ All three fused together ▪ Supports weight of upper body ▪ Protects lower abdominal organs	▪ Clavicle and scapula

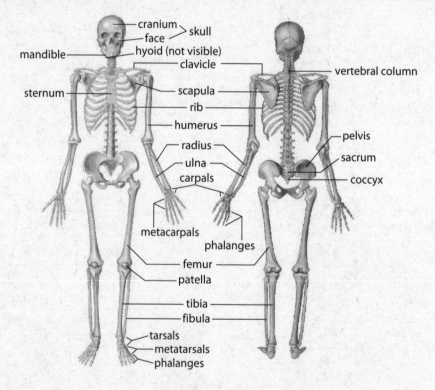

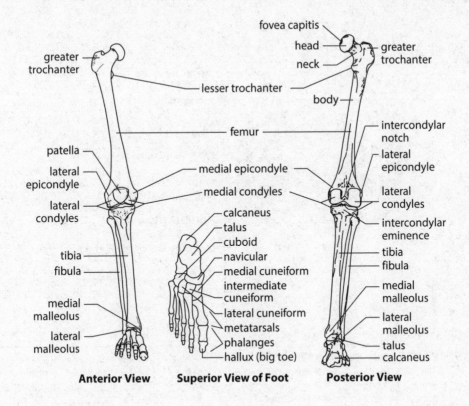

Anterior View **Superior View of Foot** **Posterior View**

Articulations

Joints or articulations are the connecting points of bone that allow movement and flexibility. Simple movements, like the bending of a finger, involve an articulation of bone. Complex movements, like those that may be required of the body during physical exercise or dance, involve a wide range of articulations operating all at once. There are a few different types of joints you should know for the HESI A2, as detailed below.

- Types of joints:

Synovial	Cartilaginous	Fibrous
■ Synovial cavity filled with synovial fluid	■ Fibro or hyaline cartilage	■ Collagen connective tissue
■ High mobility	■ Moderate mobility	■ No mobility (fixed, immovable)
■ Diarthrosis (highly movable)	■ Amphiarthrosis (some movement)	■ Synarthrosis (no movement)
■ Lubricates movement	■ Examples: Growth plates, ribs, spinal cord	■ Example: Cranial sutures
■ Most common joint		
■ Capsular ligaments common		

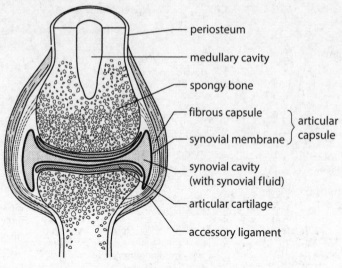

A Synovial Joint

- Movement of joints:

Ball-and-socket	Condyloid	Hinge
▪ Ball shape (head) and socket (acetabulum) ▪ Spherical shape ▪ Examples: Shoulder, femur-pelvic connection (hip)	▪ Elliptical shape ▪ Example: Wrist	▪ One degree of freedom ▪ Examples: Knee, interphalangeal joints (finger movement)
Saddle ▪ Comparable to condyloid ▪ Example: Thumb	**Pivot** ▪ Grants rotation ▪ One degree of freedom ▪ Example: Pronation and supination of forearm	

HESI Tip: There are different ways of classifying anatomy. The "degrees of freedom" mentioned under "Pivot" above is one of those ways. A higher degree of freedom means the joint is more movable in general. A lower degree of freedom means the joint is more rigid.

The Muscular System

Every movement of the human body is facilitated by the muscular system. For example, walking requires complex involvement in a number of muscles, especially in the legs. Any voluntary contraction (skeletal muscle) describes a section of the muscular system. This section explains where a muscle is found, how it is attached (originates), and the type of movement involved.

Types of Muscle

- Skeletal muscle
  - o Voluntary movement
  - o Striated (histology)
  - o Plentiful nuclei/mitochondria (ATP production)
- Cardiac muscle
  - o Involuntary movement
  - o Pulsating movement
  - o Intercalated discs: Connect individual cardiomyocytes to function as a whole organ (heart)
  - o Triggered by electrical nodes (SA node, AV node, Purkinje fibers)
- Smooth muscle
  - o Involuntary movement
  - o Thin lining of muscle
  - o Gastrointestinal tract (peristalsis), blood vessels, uterus, etc.

HESI Tip: While cardiac and smooth muscle are listed above as a general review of muscles, this section's discussion of the muscular system focuses on skeletal muscle. Cardiac muscle is part of the cardiovascular system and is covered there. Smooth muscle can be found in blood vessels and the intestines and is covered in the vascular system and digestive system sections of this chapter.

Anatomy of Muscle Tissue

- Muscle fibers (cells): Unique cells allowing movement by sliding
  - o Actin and myosin (myofibrils): Filaments sliding, causing movement
  - o Important molecules for filament sliding
    - Calcium: Electrolyte exposes binding site for actin
    - Troponin: Protein binds with calcium to reveal tropomyosin binding site
  - o Sarcolemma: Plasma membrane
  - o Sarcoplasm: Cytoplasm of muscle cell
  - o Sarcomere: Repeated sequence of myosin and actin (create striated appearance)
- Muscle fascicle: Group of muscle fibers
  - o Parallel fascicle: Found in biceps
  - o Circular fascicle: Found in mouth
  - o Pennate fascicle: Found in deltoids

HESI Tip: Muscle fibers (actin/myosin) slide over each other to create movement. They do not "contract" in the sense of balling up like clenching a fist.

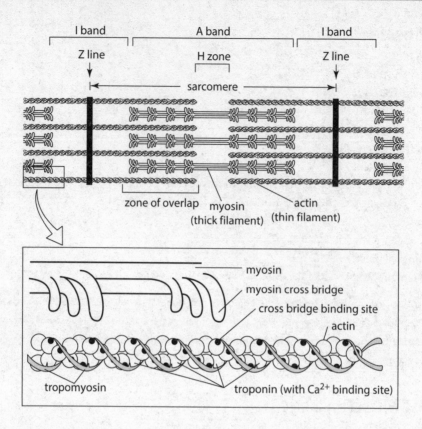

- Connective tissue
  - Endomysium: Connective tissue around singular muscle cells
  - Perimysium: Connective tissue around groups of muscle cells (fascicle)
  - Epimysium: Connective tissue around entire muscle
  - Fascia: Protective sheet of connective tissue

Motor Neurons

- Specialized neuron for muscle movement
- Acetylcholine (ACh): Neurotransmitter responsible for muscle action potentials
- Neuromuscular junction: ACh diffuses through synapse

Physiology of Muscle Tissue

- Contraction phases
  - Latent period: Calcium release
  - Contraction period: Actual movement period
  - Relaxation period: Calcium reabsorbed
  - Refractory period: Time required to reboot (second stimulus will not cause contraction)

- Strength
  - Motor neuron number: Increased number indicates increased strength
  - Strengthened by increased muscle fibers and fascicles

HESI Tip: Muscles do not grow by swelling. They grow by increasing the number of muscle filaments and fibers. This is what bodybuilders try to accomplish when lifting weights. An overall increase in muscle fiber numbers increases strength.

  - Treppe (staircase) and temporal (wave) effects
    - Repeated stimulus leading to increased strength
  - Slow twitch (fiber) muscles: Low strength, high stamina (running)
  - Fast twitch (fiber) muscles: High strength, low stamina (sprint)
- Energy for muscles
  - Molecules crucial for muscle energy
    - ATP: Basic energy molecule
    - Creatine phosphate: Aids in ATP production
    - Glucose: Stored as glycogen
    - Fatty acids: Break down to form ATP
  - Deficit of oxygen and energy (ATP, glycogen)
  - Leads to lactic acid build-up in muscles (burning sensation)

Skeletal Muscle

- Origin: Muscle point attached to bone
- Insertion: Muscle point attached to moving frame
- Belly: Center of whole muscle
- Synergist muscle: Supports primary muscle
- Antagonist muscle: Opposite movement to primary muscle

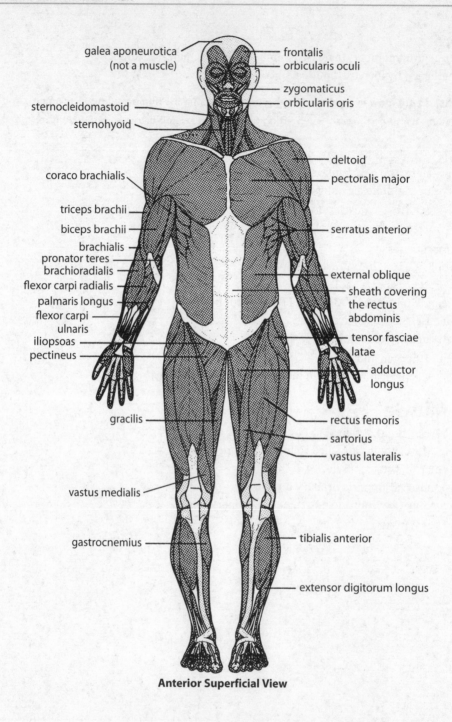

Anterior Superficial View

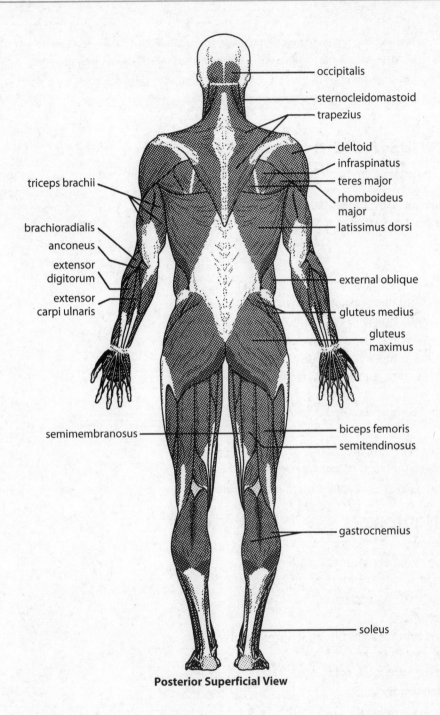

occipitalis

sternocleidomastoid

trapezius

deltoid

infraspinatus

teres major

rhomboideus major

latissimus dorsi

external oblique

gluteus medius

gluteus maximus

triceps brachii

brachioradialis

anconeus

extensor digitorum

extensor carpi ulnaris

semimembranosus

biceps femoris

semitendinosus

gastrocnemius

soleus

Posterior Superficial View

HESI Tip: Similar to memorizing bones, the process of memorizing all of the muscles is a tedious one. It is also not the best use of time when studying for the HESI A2. While learning all of the muscles can be beneficial, for the time being, focus on the major muscle groups, such as individual muscle groups throughout body areas. For example, the main muscles of the leg include the quadriceps, hamstrings, and adductor muscles.

The Nervous System

An enormous and complicated collection of nerves, the brain, and the spinal cord make up the human nervous system. This network receives, interprets, and reacts to all types of information communicated to and from the human body. From interpreting speech to managing blood pressure, from feeling pain to feeling happiness—every piece of information the human body is exposed to is processed through the nervous system.

Neurons

- Cell body: Contains nucleus and organelles
- Dendrite: Branched arms of cell body
  o Receives stimuli
- Axon: Skinny long thread of cell
  o Transmits stimuli down cell thread
  o Trigger zone (initiates action potential)
  o Myelin sheath (speeds up action potential)
- Synapse
  o End structure of neuron
  o Neurotransmitters transmit via chemical signal
- Nissl bodies: Rough endoplasmic reticulum cluster

Types of Neurons

- Motor neurons
  o Efferent neurons transmitting motor signals
  o Transmit from the central nervous system (CNS)
  o Examples: Muscles, glands
- Sensory neurons
  o Afferent neurons transmitting sensory signals
  o Receive signals to the CNS
  o Examples: Pain, heat, cold, touch
- Association neurons
  o Interneurons inside the CNS
  o Transmit sensory and motor signals
  o Most common neurons in the body

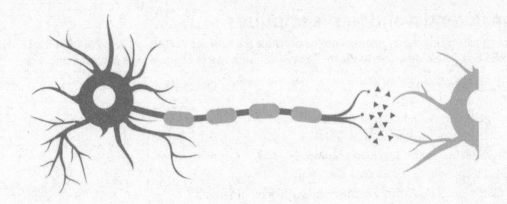

Neuroglia

- Glia cells assist and preserve neurons.
- Astrocytes
  - Govern exchange of ions and materials between blood and neurons
- Oligodendrocytes
  - Insulate with myelin sheath in CNS
- Schwann cells
  - Insulate with myelin sheath in peripheral nervous system (PNS)
  - Aid conduction of action potential and regeneration of cells
- Microglia
  - Type of macrophage destroying pathogens and waste by phagocytosis
- Ependymal cells
  - Produce cerebrospinal fluid (CSF)
  - Surround ventricles in the brain

HESI Tip: Dysfunction of the myelin sheath occurs in certain diseases. Multiple sclerosis (MS) is an example of one of those diseases. It falls in the category of demyelinating diseases. Patients can lose functions of muscle and sensory organs. This displays the importance of Schwann cells and the resulting protective and insulating sheath.

Types of Sensory Receptors

Nociceptors	Mechanoreceptors	Photoreceptors
- Pain	- Touch - Sound	- Light - Cones (color) - Rods (no color)
Chemoreceptors	Thermoreceptors	Pressoreceptors
- Chemical changes - Blood pH, smell, etc.	- Temperature	- Blood pressure - Example: Carotid artery

HESI Tip: Some other specialized sensory receptors interpret other types of stimuli: Gustatory receptors taste. Olfactory receptors smell.

Action Potential and Nerve Impulses

Electrical signals produced by neurons are responsible for how the nervous system communicates with other parts of the body. This electricity is created by the fast movement of molecules across membranes.

- Sodium-potassium pump
  - Polarization
    - Sodium: Outside of membrane
    - Potassium: Inside of membrane
    - Negative charge inside of membrane
    - Positive charge outside of membrane
  - Gated channels: Open to neurotransmitters or stimuli
- Phases of an action potential
  - Depolarization: Sodium gates flood open in a domino effect down the axon
  - Repolarization: Potassium gates open
  - Hyperpolarization: Excess potassium slips outside of the membrane
  - Refractory period: Membrane potential finds baseline

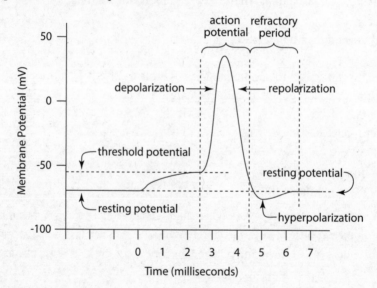

- Neurotransmitters
  - Excitatory: Increases possibility for action potential
  - Inhibitory: Decreases possibility for action potential
  - Types of neurotransmitters:

Acetylcholine (ACh): Motor neurons and glands	Dopamine/serotonin: Mood	Epinephrine/norepinephrine: Autonomic nervous system
Histamine: Immune response in mast cells	Glutamate: Most common in brain and spinal cord	GABA: Inhibitory and sedation

HESI Tip: There are more than 50 identified neurotransmitters in total with vast functions and effects. Those listed in the table above are the most common.

Two-Part Nervous System

- Central nervous system (CNS)
  - Brain and spinal cord
- Peripheral nervous system (PNS)
  - Outside CNS
  - Efferent: Away from brain
  - Afferent: Toward brain

Effector Classification

- Autonomic nervous system
  - Sympathetic
    - Stimulation body actions
    - Fight-or-flight response
      - Increased heart rate
      - Increased sugar release
      - Pupillary dilation
  - Parasympathetic
    - Relaxation body actions
      - Digestive function
      - Urination and defecation
      - Sexual arousal
- Somatic nervous system
  - Motor movement (skeletal muscle)

HESI Tip: The sympathetic and parasympathetic nervous systems work opposite each other to balance and maintain body homeostasis.

The Brain

- Areas of the brain:

Forebrain (prosencephalon)	Midbrain (mesencephalon)	Hindbrain (rhombencephalon)

  - Cerebrum
    - Left and right hemispheres
    - Corpus callosum: Connects hemispheres
    - Lobes
      - Frontal, parietal, temporal, occipital, and cerebellum
    - Gyrus (ridge) and sulcus (grooves)
  - Ventricles
    - Four total ventricles
    - Release cerebrospinal fluid (CSF)
  - White matter: Myelinated axons
  - Grey matter: Unmyelinated axons

- o Blood-brain barrier
  - Protects the brain from pathogens
  - Decreased membrane permeability (tight junctions)

Other Important Areas of the Brain		
Thalamus ■ Sensory information	**Hypothalamus** ■ Emotion, body temperature, etc. ■ Antidiuretic hormone production ■ Oxytocin production	**Epithalamus** ■ Pineal gland (sleep)
Brainstem ■ Connects brain to spinal cord ■ Midbrain and pons ■ Medulla oblongata (heart rate and breathing)	**Hippocampus** ■ In temporal lobe ■ Limbic system (emotion)	**Cerebellum** ■ Balance and coordination ■ Reticular activation system (consciousness)

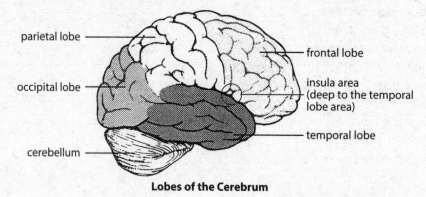

Lobes of the Cerebrum

Meninges

- Protective sheet surrounding the brain and spinal cord
- Layers of meninges:

Dura mater	Arachnoid mater	Pia mater
■ Outermost layer ■ Subdural (below the dura)	■ Middle layer ■ Subarachnoid (below the arachnoid)	■ Inside layer

The Spinal Cord

- 31 pairs of nerves
- Four plexus systems:

Cervical plexus	Brachial plexus
■ Innervates neck and partial trunk	■ Innervates arms and partial trunk
Lumbar plexus	**Sacral plexus**
■ Innervates anterior thigh	■ Innervates posterior thigh and leg

HESI Tip: A plexus is a network of nerves coming to and from certain areas of the body. It is worth noting that there is no thoracic plexus.

The Endocrine System

The release of hormones throughout the body by glands and organs regulates a vast number of essential body processes. In teaming up with the nervous system, homeostasis can be achieved. Hormones, or chemical molecules, instruct certain cells to perform specific functions. These effects are accomplished by hormones moving throughout our bloodstream and being able to communicate with the body as a whole. Many of these hormones can last hours to days, much longer than nervous system effects.

Types of Hormones

- Steroids
- Nonsteroidal
  - Polypeptides (protein)
  - Amino acids
  - Eicosanoids: Affect nearby cells

HESI Tip: While steroid hormones have more of a direct effect on the cell itself and the DNA, nonsteroidal hormones affect adenosine monophosphate (AMP) to communicate to the cell about protein production, the speed at which something is made.

Endocrine Glands

Pituitary gland	Hypothalamus
<ul><li>Anterior lobe<ul><li>Tropic hormones (influence other glands)</li><li>Thyroid-stimulating hormone (TSH)</li><li>Adrenocorticotropic hormone (ACTH)</li><li>Somatotropin or growth hormone (GH)</li><li>Follicle-stimulating hormone (FSH)</li></ul></li><li>Posterior lobe<ul><li>Oxytocin and antidiuretic hormone (ADH)</li></ul></li></ul>	<ul><li>Prompts other glands to release hormones</li><li>Connects to pituitary gland at infundibulum</li><li>Observes homeostasis and reacts when needed</li></ul>
Thyroid/parathyroid gland	**Adrenal glands**
<ul><li>Involved in metabolism</li><li>Thyroxine (T4)</li><li>Calcitonin</li><li>Parathyroid hormone</li></ul>	<ul><li>Adrenaline and noradrenaline</li><li>Mineralocorticoids</li><li>Glucocorticoids<ul><li>Cortisol (stress hormone): Releases glucose and histamines</li></ul></li><li>Androgens</li></ul>
Ovaries/testes	**Pancreas**
<ul><li>Testosterone</li><li>Estrogen</li><li>Progesterone</li></ul>	<ul><li>Islets of Langerhans (contain specialized cells)</li><li>Insulin (released from beta cells)<ul><li>Causes glucose consumption</li></ul></li><li>Glucagon (released from alpha cells)<ul><li>Causes glucose release from liver</li></ul></li></ul>

HESI Tip: The full list of hormones utilized by the human body, where they come from, and how they work is for more advanced study of endocrinology. Remember to keep it simple and stick to the basics for the HESI A2.

The Cardiovascular System

Undoubtedly one of the most researched and talked-about body systems, the cardiovascular system may get all of this attention because when part of it is malfunctioning, the effects become apparent. A patient may become short of breath or dizzy. For the purpose of the HESI A2 (and future classes), focus on form and function. The cardiovascular system includes the heart and blood vessels and the blood itself.

Components of Blood

- Formed elements (45% of whole blood):

Red blood cells (RBCs)	White blood cells (WBCs)	Platelets

■ Carry oxygen by hemoglobin
■ Reticulocytes (baby RBCs)
  o Developed in bone marrow
■ Erythrocytes (adult RBCs)
  o No nucleus
  o 90–120 day lifespan
	■ Immune system function
	■ Neutrophils (most abundant)
	■ Lymphocytes (T and B cells)
	■ Leukocytes
	■ Eosinophils
	■ Basophils (allergic response)
	■ Monocytes/macrophages
		■ Clotting function (coagulation)
		■ Thrombocytes
		  o Developed in bone marrow
		  o No nucleus

HESI Tip: As discussed in the skeletal system, hematopoiesis (the process of making formed elements of the blood) occurs in the red bone marrow of long bones such as the femur. Hematopoietic stem cells become specific elements like RBCs or platelets. Erythropoietin is a hormone released by the kidneys to encourage this process, specifically erythropoiesis (the production of RBCs).

- Plasma (55% of whole blood)
  - o Roughly 90% water

Proteins	Electrolytes	Waste
■ Albumin ■ Globulins ■ Fibrinogen	■ Sodium (Na^+) ■ Potassium (K^+) ■ Calcium (Ca^{2+}) ■ Magnesium (Mg^{2+})	■ Creatinine ■ Urea ■ Bilirubin

HESI Tip: As with much of anatomy and physiology, the components of blood include many more things than are listed above. Understand the foundation first. Lab values and what these components mean for your patients will be covered in your future nursing classes.

The Heart

- Two circuits of blood flow:

Systemic circuit	Pulmonary circuit
■ Blood pumps through entire body minus lungs. ■ Blood pumped out of the left ventricle	■ Blood pumps to lungs and back to heart. ■ Blood pumped out of right ventricle

- Anatomy of the heart
  - Atria and ventricles
    - Atria receive blood.
    - Ventricles pump blood out.
    - Left ventricle is the strongest.
  - Tricuspid and bicuspid valves
    - Between atria and ventricles
    - Tricuspid on right
    - Bicuspid on left
  - Semilunar valves (aortic and pulmonic)
- Cardiac cycle
  - Systole: Contraction phase
    - Blood ejects
  - Diastole: Relaxation phase
    - Blood fills
- Conductive system
  - Autorhythmic nodes (pacemaker cells)
    - Sinoatrial node (SA): Primary trigger
    - Atrioventricular node (AV)
    - Purkinje fibers
  - Transmits through myocardium (heart muscle)
  - Electrocardiogram (ECG or EKG) displays the heart's conduction system.

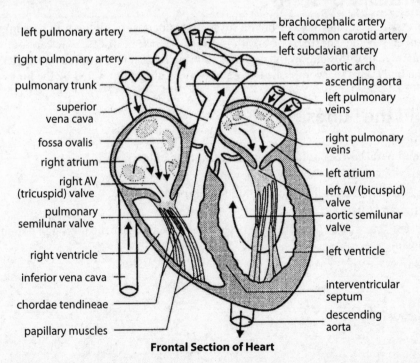

Frontal Section of Heart

HESI Tip: It is important to understand the flow of blood through the heart, and to know if the blood is oxygenated or deoxygenated. For example, arteries are typically considered to carry oxygen, which is true; however, the pulmonary artery does not. "Artery" simply means blood flowing away from the heart.

The Vascular System

- Blood vessels:

Arteries	Veins
■ Deliver blood away from heart	■ Transport blood back to the heart
■ Aorta (largest artery)	■ Vena cava (largest vein)
■ Arterioles (smallest arteries)	■ Thin
■ Muscular (smooth muscle)	■ Contain valves (prevent backflow)
■ Elastic (expand to handle pressure)	

- Capillaries
    - Exchange of molecules with cells
        - Gases (oxygen and carbon dioxide)
        - Water, nutrients, waste, etc.

HESI Tip: Smooth muscle in the arteries allows for vasoconstriction and vasodilation and contributes to the regulation of blood pressure and blood flow.

The Respiratory System

Anyone who has experienced shortness of breath (dyspnea) understands all too well how important the respiratory system is. Whether shortness of breath is due to exercise or disease, one cannot live without breathing. The main goal of this important system is to bring oxygen into the body and release carbon dioxide out of the body. This is accomplished by a pathway of airways powered by the lungs.

Airways and the Lungs

- Upper airway
    - Mouth and nasal cavities bring gases to and from the lungs.
    - Epiglottis protects airways during swallowing.
    - Trachea (windpipe) branches into right and left bronchi.
    - Humidifies and filters air
        - Cilia: Tiny hairs catch unwanted particles, which are then expelled through coughing or swallowing
- Lower airway
    - Lungs
    - Bronchi
    - Bronchioles
    - Alveoli

- Lungs
  - Right lung: Three lobes
  - Left lung: Two lobes
  - Pleural cavity encloses the lungs (contains pleural fluid).

The Gases

- Oxygen: Carried by hemoglobin
  - Higher hemoglobin saturation than carbon dioxide
- Carbon dioxide: Carried by hemoglobin
  - Smaller hemoglobin saturation than oxygen
  - Regulates blood pH (hydrogen ions)
  - Converts to bicarbonate when used

Respiration

- External respiration
  - Ventilation: Exchange of oxygen and carbon dioxide in the alveoli (lungs)
  - Inhalation: Breathing in oxygen
    - Active muscle use (diaphragm and external intercostal muscles)
  - Exhalation: Breathing out carbon dioxide
    - Relaxation of diaphragm and lungs
  - Medulla (brain) controls breathing by chemoreceptors.
- Internal respiration
  - Gas exchange at the cellular level (blood, interstitial fluids, cells)
  - ATP production requires oxygen.

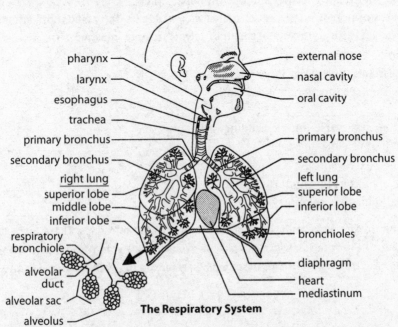

pharynx — external nose
larynx — nasal cavity
esophagus — oral cavity
trachea
primary bronchus — primary bronchus
secondary bronchus — secondary bronchus
right lung — left lung
superior lobe — superior lobe
middle lobe — inferior lobe
inferior lobe
respiratory bronchiole — bronchioles
alveolar duct — diaphragm
alveolar sac — heart
alveolus — mediastinum

The Respiratory System

The Digestive System

From mouth to anus, the entire gastrointestinal tract is one continuous tube, the alimentary canal. How food is digested and absorbed is the job of the digestive system as a whole. It would be worthwhile to refresh macromolecule knowledge such as differences between carbohydrates, lipids, proteins, and nucleic acids. This information can be found in Chapter 5, "Biology Review." Energy for the human body comes from food; food is made up of macromolecules. Build from, and on, existing knowledge—always.

Upper GI Tract

- Mouth
  - Tongue: Mechanically moves food
  - Teeth: 32 permanent perform mastication (chewing)
  - Saliva: Released by three glands, contains digestive enzymes
  - Taste buds (papillae)
- Esophagus
  - Moves food bolus by peristalsis (wavelike movement of smooth muscle)
- Stomach
  - Mucosal lining: Protects stomach from tissue breakdown
  - Goblet cells: Produce mucus and hydrochloric acid
  - Hydrochloric acid: Aids in food breakdown (food becomes chyme)
  - Intrinsic factor: Aids in vitamin B12 absorption

Lower GI Tract

- Small intestine
  - Duodenum: Pancreatic enzymes and bile from liver enter
  - Jejunum: Absorption of important nutrients such as sugars, fatty acids, and amino acids occurs
  - Ileum: Ileocecal valve controls movement of chyme to large intestine
- Large intestine
  - Cecum: Beginning portion of large intestine
  - Appendix: Immune function, not digestion
  - Colon
    - Ascending, transverse, and descending
    - Largest part of large intestine
  - Rectum and anal canal
    - Interior sphincter: Involuntary
    - External sphincter: Voluntary

HESI Tip: Villi and microvilli are important anatomical features of the intestines. These tiny extensions off of the mucosal lining increase the surface area of tissue available to absorb nutrients. Without this feature, the human body would not be able to absorb enough nutrients to sustain bodily functions, which could lead to diseases and disorders.

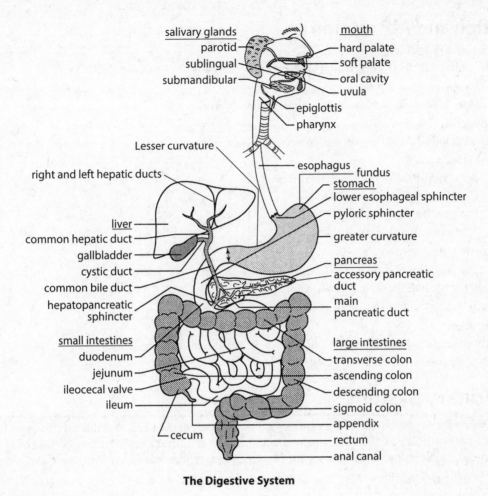

salivary glands
- parotid
- sublingual
- submandibular

mouth
- hard palate
- soft palate
- oral cavity
- uvula
- epiglottis
- pharynx

Lesser curvature

right and left hepatic ducts

esophagus
fundus
stomach
lower esophageal sphincter
pyloric sphincter

liver
common hepatic duct
gallbladder
cystic duct
common bile duct
hepatopancreatic sphincter

greater curvature

pancreas
accessory pancreatic duct
main pancreatic duct

small intestines
- duodenum
- jejunum
- ileocecal valve
- ileum

cecum

large intestines
- transverse colon
- ascending colon
- descending colon
- sigmoid colon
- appendix
- rectum
- anal canal

The Digestive System

The Pancreas

- Enzyme production for chemical digestion
  - Amylase, lipase, proteases, etc.
- Pancreatic juice
  - Enzymes and bicarbonate mixture
  - Enters into the duodenum

The Liver and Gallbladder

- Production of bile (made of bilirubin and cholesterol)
- Bile aids in the breakdown of lipids.
- Filtration
  - Toxic molecules, RBCs, WBCs, bacteria, ammonia, etc.
  - Performed by Kupffer cells
- Gallbladder stores extra bile.

Digestion and Absorption

- Mechanical digestion
  - Breakdown of food into smaller segments mechanically
  - Chewing
  - Tossing in stomach and small intestine (segmentation)
- Chemical digestion
  - Breakdown of food into smaller molecules chemically
  - Enzymes
    - Amylases: Break down carbohydrates
    - Proteases: Break down proteins
    - Lipases: Break down lipids (fats)
    - Nucleases: Break down nucleic acids
- Digestive hormones
  - Cholecystokinin: Stimulates discharge of bile and pancreatic juice
  - Gastrin: Stimulates discharge of hydrochloric acid
  - Secretin: Stimulates bile production
- Absorption
  - Absorbed nutrients in the blood flow through hepatic portal vein to liver.
  - Liver cleans out harmful particles.

The Urinary System

While the vast majority of humans have experienced the sensation and need to urinate daily, except for dialysis patients potentially, we are unaware of the immensely important underlying processes of the urinary system. Regulating blood pressure, filtering the blood, and excreting potentially toxic materials are all actions of the urinary system.

The Kidneys

- Left kidney slightly superior to (above) the right kidney
- Reside in retroperitoneal space
- Segments of the kidneys:

Renal cortex	Renal medulla	Renal sinus
- Outer area - Cortical nephrons	- Medullary pyramids - Juxtamedullary nephrons	- Connects to ureters - Renal arteries and veins enter and leave.

  - Nephrons
    - Filtration of blood by glomeruli inside Bowman's capsule
      - Water, solutes, etc.
      - RBCs not permitted to pass
      - Water reabsorption
    - Filtration occurs by hydrostatic pressure (blood pressure).
    - More than a million nephrons per kidney

o Renal tubules
- Excrete urine (waste) from kidneys to bladder
  - Urea, creatinine, ammonia, medications, etc.
- Reabsorption of molecules and ions
  - Water, nutrients, electrolytes, etc.
  - Antidiuretic hormone (ADH) stimulates water reabsorption.

Ureters, Bladder, and Urethra

Ureters	Bladder	Urethra
■ Transports urine from kidneys to bladder	■ Stores urine ■ Transitional cells allow expansion. ■ Stretch receptors stimulate desire to urinate.	■ Drains urine out of body ■ Longer urethra in males ■ Passes prostate in males

Renal Hormones

- Erythropoietin: Stimulates bone marrow production of RBCs
- Renin: Aids in blood pressure regulation
- Calcitriol: Promotes calcium absorption

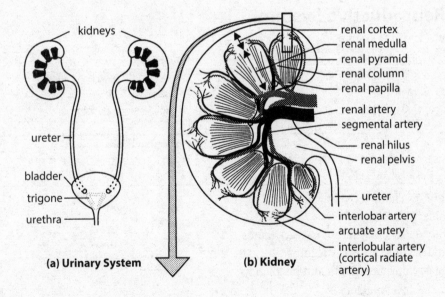

(a) Urinary System   (b) Kidney

The Reproductive System

Without reproduction, no organism or species could survive. It is essential to make copies, or offspring, to proliferate the species. The action of how reproduction is possible is covered by this body system. The study of how a fetus is carried and delivered is covered in nursing school.

Male Reproductive System

- Components of the system:

Scrotum	Penis	Testes
- Encompasses testes - Outside of body for temperature regulation	- Delivery of sperm and urine - Dilation of arteries during erection	- Spermatogenesis (sperm production) - Seminiferous tubules (site of spermatogenesis) - Secrete testosterone and androgens
Epididymis	Prostate	Sperm
- Storage of sperm - Vas deferens - Push sperm forward toward urethra	- Releases milky substance (semen) to nourish sperm	- Haploid (half) cells, no pairs of chromosomes - 23 chromosomes each - Flagellum tail propels

- Secondary sex characteristics
  - Hair growth (facial, body, pubic)
  - Muscle growth
  - Deepening of voice

Female Reproductive System

- Components of the system:

Uterus	Ovaries
- Hollow organ that carries child - Fundus (upper) - Cervix opens to vagina. - Myometrium allows contractions during labor.	- Oogenesis (egg production) - Begins in fetal development - Follicle encases the egg.
Vagina	Fallopian tubes
- Sperm enter through sexual intercourse. - Delivery of infant during labor.	- Carry the egg to uterus - Cilia (little hairs) push egg forward.

- Secondary sex characteristics
  - Mammary glands
    - Specialized sudoriferous (sweat) glands
    - Produce milk for breastfeeding
    - Enlarge during puberty and pregnancy
  - Fat tissue development
  - Pelvic enlargement
  - Growth of body hair

- Menstruation
  - Activated each month
  - Prompted by hypothalamus and pituitary gland:
    - Release of gonadotropin (begins the menstrual cycle)
    - Release of follicle-stimulating hormone (triggers follicle development)
    - Release of luteinizing hormone (triggers ovulation)
    - Release of estrogen (rises rapidly during menstruation)
    - Release of progesterone (triggers endometrium development)
  - Ovulation: Release of the egg by the ovary

Practice Quiz

1. Using anatomical terminology, which of the following correctly describes an injury on the top of the foot?

    A. The injury is distal to the ankle.
    B. The injury is superior to the knee.
    C. The injury is ventral to the cranium.
    D. The injury is lateral to the hips.

2. After visiting an emergency room, a rotator cuff tear is discovered, specifically the tendons. Which of the following statements about tendons is correct?

    A. Tendons attach muscle to muscle.
    B. Tendons attach bone to bone.
    C. Tendons are made up of adipose tissue.
    D. Tendons are made up of collagen connective tissue.

3. Cigarette smoking is known to destroy the cilia-lined epithelium in the airways. Why is this a problem?

    A. Cilia promote oxygen absorption in the lungs.
    B. Cilia help clean the lungs of unwanted particles.
    C. Cilia release protective mucus.
    D. Cilia absorb carbon dioxide for the body.

4. The average human sheds the outermost layer of skin every 3 weeks. What is this layer called?

    A. Stratum germinativum
    B. Stratum corneum
    C. Stratum granulosum
    D. Stratum lucidum

5. Which of the following tissues helps push chyme through the gastrointestinal tract?

    A. Skeletal muscle
    B. Connective
    C. Epithelial
    D. Smooth muscle

6. A neurosurgeon has diagnosed a patient with a fracture in the lumbar spine. Which of the following describes where this fracture is located?

    A. The lower back
    B. The upper back
    C. The neck
    D. The brainstem

7. What is the name of the tube in the scrotum that propels sperm during ejaculation? The tube is commonly clipped in a procedure for male birth control.

   A.   Seminiferous tubules
   B.   Epididymis
   C.   Vas deferens
   D.   Urethra

8. Where do pancreatic enzymes and bile enter into the gastrointestinal tract?

   A.   Stomach
   B.   Duodenum
   C.   Jejunum
   D.   Cecum

9. What part of the respiratory system is responsible for the exchange of gases (oxygen and carbon dioxide)?

   A.   Alveoli
   B.   Bronchi
   C.   Trachea
   D.   Diaphragm

10. Which gland is largely responsible for the regulation of calcium within our bodies?

   A.   Thyroid gland
   B.   Adrenal glands
   C.   Pituitary gland
   D.   Parathyroid gland

11. While listening to a patient's heart, a cardiologist notices a murmur of the tricuspid valve. Where is the tricuspid valve in the human heart?

   A.   The right side of the heart, between the atria and ventricle
   B.   The right side of the heart, between the vena cava and atria
   C.   The left side of the heart, between the atria and ventricle
   D.   The left side of the heart, between the ventricle and aorta

12. Which of the following is the correct order of the meninges, from outermost to innermost layer?

   A.   Pia, arachnoid, dura
   B.   Pia, dura, arachnoid
   C.   Arachnoid, dura, pia
   D.   Dura, arachnoid, pia

13. A sunburn is typically described as superficial. What does "superficial" mean here?

   A. The burn is through multiple layers of skin.
   B. The burn penetrates into deep layers of skin.
   C. The burn is isolated to the top layers of the skin.
   D. The burn has destroyed muscle and capillaries.

14. Where on the human body would you find the zygomatic bone?

   A. The cranium
   B. The chest
   C. The face
   D. The ears

15. Before nutrients absorbed by the gastrointestinal tract (GI) move to systemic blood flow, they move through the portal vein. Where is the portal vein?

   A. The liver
   B. The pancreas
   C. The kidneys
   D. The lungs

Answer Explanations

1. **A.** Distal means away from the center of the body, so the foot is distal to the ankle and anything higher up on the leg, choice A. Superior (choice B) means toward the head of the body, so the injury is not higher up than the knee. Describing something as ventral (choice C) or dorsal to another body part would be incorrect. Ventral simply means "the front," whereas dorsal means "the back." In this case, the injury on top of the foot would be described as dorsal. Lateral (choice D) means to the side of or farther from the middle. The hips are lateral to begin with, so something could not be more lateral than something that is already as far lateral as possible. This can be confusing; the best way to learn is to practice looking at a human body and describing these scenarios out loud.

2. **D.** The rotator cuff is in the shoulder, and is a frequent site of injury given its repeated use by the human body. Tendons are made up of strong connective tissue, mostly collagen, choice D. They are also mainly responsible for attaching muscle to bone, not muscle to muscle (choice A) or bone to bone (choice B). Some tendons also attach to structures, like the eyeball. Tendons are not made up of adipose tissue (choice C), commonly known as body fat.

3. **B.** Cilia are tiny hairs that line portions of the epithelium of the airways. They wave back and forth to clean the lungs, choice B, along with specialized mucus that catches the unwanted particles. When cilia are destroyed, it can lead to disease and further respiratory problems. Cilia are not involved in gas exchange of oxygen (choice A) or carbon dioxide (choice D). Cilia work with secretory cells that release mucus, but they do not release mucus themselves (choice C).

4. **B.** The stratum corneum, choice B, is the outermost layer of skin that is shed. This layer of skin is completely keratinized and dead. Stratum lucidum (choice D) is the next layer below corneum; it is specialized for thick areas of the skin like the soles of the hands and feet. Stratum granulosum (choice C) is where keratin is made and integrated into the skin. Stratum germinativum (choice A), also called the basal layer, is where mitosis occurs and a proliferation of new skin cells replenishes the old.

5. **D.** Smooth muscle, choice D, around the gastrointestinal (GI) tract performs peristalsis, the wavelike movement propelling food or chyme forward. It is an involuntary process. Skeletal muscle (choice A) is voluntary, where we choose our movements. Connective tissue (choice B) supports and protects the body. Epithelial tissue (choice C) lines areas of the body. For example, epithelial tissue lines the GI tract, but it is not responsible for the forward movement of chyme; it acts to digest and absorb.

6. **A.** The lumbar spine is in the lower half of the back, choice A. The cervical spine is the highest point on the spine connecting to the brainstem and brain. The brainstem itself is not a part of the spine. The thoracic spine is in the upper back. Below the lumbar spine is the sacral vertebrae and then the coccyx. Understand the order of the spine from the top down; cervical, thoracic, lumbar, sacral, coccyx.

7. **C.** The vas deferens, choice C, carries sperm away from the epididymis and toward the ejaculatory ducts. During ejaculation, the smooth muscle around the vas deferens contracts, pushing the sperm forward. The seminiferous tubules (choice A) exist in the testes and produce sperm. The epididymis (choice B) connects the testes and the vas deferens; it is used for storage of sperm. The urethra (choice D) carries urine and semen (containing sperm); in a male, the urethra is extended outward on the penis and is not in the scrotum.

8. **B.** The duodenum (choice B), or the first portion of the small intestine directly after the stomach, has pancreatic juices and bile released into it. The liver, as it releases bile, and the pancreas, with digestive enzymes in the juice, are released in a duct system that releases directly into the duodenum upon stimulation. The stomach (choice A) releases the enzyme pepsin, along with other substances such as

hydrochloric acid. The jejunum (choice C) is the portion of the small intestine after the duodenum; it does not have bile or pancreatic juices released within it. The cecum (choice D) is the first portion of the large intestine; it also does not have bile or pancreatic juices released within it.

9. **A.** At the very end of the respiratory tract, the bronchioles terminate into alveoli. These grapelike sacs, called alveolar sacs, are wrapped with multiple capillaries. The alveoli, choice A, are where the exchange of oxygen and carbon dioxide, with blood, occurs. The airways themselves do not exchange gases, such as the bronchi (choice B) and trachea (choice C). The diaphragm (choice D), though hugely important for breathing, is not technically a part of the respiratory system. It is a muscle that aids in breathing.

10. **D.** The parathyroid gland, choice D, is largely responsible for calcium regulation in our bodies. Problems with the parathyroid can affect blood levels and calcium and eventually may cause bone issues. The thyroid gland (choice A) regulates body metabolism. The adrenal glands (choice B) release steroids and adrenaline. The pituitary gland (choice C), often referred to as a master gland, oversees numerous body processes, but not the regulation of calcium.

11. **A.** The tricuspid valve, one of the atrioventricular valves, is on the right side of the heart between the atria and ventricle, choice A. The bicuspid valve, also called the mitral valve, is on the left side of the heart. It is crucial to understand the flow of blood through the heart and the names for all of these components. The aortic valve moves blood out of the left ventricle and into the aorta. It is on the left side of the heart. The atria do not have valves where the blood enters.

12. **D.** The outermost layer of the meninges is the dura mater. Beneath the dura is the arachnoid mater. Beneath the arachnoid is the pia mater. Therefore, choice D is correct. While this question is fairly straightforward, more advanced knowledge regarding the meninges comes into play with diseases and patient issues.

13. **C.** "Superficial" describes something on the outside of the body. Therefore, the burn is isolated to the top layers of the skin, choice C. The opposite of superficial would be "deep," so the other answer choices do not make sense. A superficial sunburn is not deep (choice B) or responsible for the destruction of multiple layers of skin (choice A). A sunburn does not destroy muscle or blood vessels (choice D). Remember, skin has three layers total. Most sunburns do not even penetrate the first layer, the epidermis.

14. **C.** The zygomatic bone is one of the facial bones, choice C. It makes up the arch of the cheek. The cranium (choice A), or skull, has multiple bones fused at sutures; it does not contain the zygomatic bone. The chest (choice B) contains bones like the sternum and ribcage. The ears (choice D) have three small bones: the stapes (stirrup), malleus (hammer), and incus (anvil). Collectively, they are called ossicles.

15. **A.** The portal vein brings blood back to the liver, choice A, to be filtered out. This causes anything absorbed to be filtered and cleaned before it enters full circulation of the human body, from nutrients to medications. The organs in the other answer choices do not host the portal vein.

Chapter 8

Physics Review

The physics section on the HESI A2 contains 25 questions.

Physics can be a difficult subject to master; luckily, the HESI A2 does not require you to be a rocket scientist. Just the basics of physics are required here. How does matter move? How does matter behave? In addition, understanding the laws of pressure and volume is important in cardiology and other body systems, as well as concepts of physics underlying diagnostic techniques. It is not uncommon for people to be apprehensive about this topic because of a potential lack of understanding of the math that is involved. Mathematics is not covered in this book, but in the answer explanations to the practice quiz questions at the end of the chapter, the math used to solve the problems is shown for your reference. It may be helpful for you to review a resource that could assist you with the math before you focus on the particulars of physics. Algebra is commonly used when formulating and solving the math problems within this subject.

Important note: Not all nursing programs require physics for application. Be sure to check which sections of the HESI A2 are required by your school before you apply or take the HESI A2. It is important to focus on the topics specific to your exam.

International System of Units (SI)

Science topics in general utilize the International System of Units (SI). While the United States as a whole has not adopted SI units or the metric system, it is the favored system of measurement in scientific and medical communities. Below is an overview of the units with their associated symbol.

Base Units

Simple Single Unit Measurements		
Unit	**Symbol**	**Definition**
second	s	time
meter	m	length
kilogram	kg	mass
ampere	A	electric current

Derived Units

- Combination of two or more base units
  - Example: Newton = $kg \cdot m \cdot s^{-2}$

Derived Units		
Unit	**Symbol**	**Definition**
newton	N	force
radian	rad	plane angle
joule	J	energy
hertz	Hz	frequency
watt	W	power
coulomb	C	electric charge
volt	V	voltage
ohm	Ω	resistance

Motion in Physics

How matter moves in our universe is one of the fundamental concepts of physics. When answering physics questions, remember to pay close attention to the units being used. It may be necessary to change a unit, such as converting minutes to seconds or feet to meters.

The metric system is covered in more detail in the appendix (pp. 155–156).

Scalar Quantity

- Magnitude, not direction (simple value number)
- Describes volume of matter
- Speed, length, area, volume, mass, density, etc.

Vector Quantity

- Magnitude and direction: More than one unit of measurement
- Describes movement/force of matter
- Velocity, displacement, momentum, force, etc.

HESI Tip: Being able to differentiate between a scalar quantity and a vector quantity is an easy beginner's strategy to understanding physics concepts.

Velocity

- Average speed
  - How fast matter is moving
  - Distance traveled divided by time to travel

$$\text{average speed} = \frac{\text{distance}}{\text{time}}, \text{ or } s = \frac{d}{t}$$

  - Cross-multiplication math

- Average velocity
  - o Do not confuse with average speed
  - o Rate during change in position (displacement)

$$\text{average velocity} = \frac{\text{final position} - \text{starting position}}{\text{final time} - \text{starting time}}$$

Acceleration

- How fast matter is speeding up
- Vector quantity
  - o Example: Meters per second

velocity = v	time = t

$$\text{average acceleration} = \frac{\Delta v}{\Delta t}$$

Note: The Δ symbol means "change in." So the formula for average acceleration is the change in velocity divided by the change in time.

Displacement

- Distance traveled by an object
- Vector quantity
- Final position minus starting position

Linear Motion

- Change in position

distance = d	velocity = v	time = t

$$d = vt$$

Projectile Motion

- Describes motion of object falling in air
- Object reacts to gravity.
- Ignores wind resistance (drag)
- Gravity acceleration (g) = 9.8 meters per second squared ÷ 32 feet per second squared or $g = \dfrac{9.8 \text{ m/s}^2}{32 \text{ ft/s}^2}$.

HESI Tip: In projectile motion, the horizontal velocity of an object is constant. The moving component is the vertical acceleration. This is calculated by using gravity acceleration, described above. Many examples describe this motion by explaining a rock thrown from a cliff. The rock will move in two directions: horizontally and vertically (falling toward the earth).

- Starting vertical velocity = 0 (if the object is standing still at the start)

$$\text{vertical velocity} = \text{starting vertical velocity} - g \times \text{time}$$

HESI Tip: The exam may ask you to calculate more than just the vertical velocity. It may ask how far an object would travel if thrown from a cliff or similar scenarios. To find the answer, the question must provide the horizontal speed of the object. Multiply this speed by the amount of time the object is in the air.

Newton's Laws of Motion

Force is a vector quantity and the center of Newtonian physics of motion. Force is a push or pull on an object. If an object has two equal forces acting on it from both directions, the two forces cancel each other out and the object does not move.

Force

- Vector quantity (magnitude and direction)
- Causes movement of an object (acceleration)
- Multiple forces may be present.

$$\text{net force} = \text{summation of forces on an object}$$

First Law of Motion

- Inertia
  - Objects at rest stay at rest.
  - Objects in motion stay in motion.
- Influences kinematics: Motion that has no cause
- Above is true unless an outside force is met.
  - Air resistance, friction, etc.

Second Law of Motion

- Acceleration is proportional to incoming force and mass.
- Influences dynamics: Motion that has a cause
- Force = mass × acceleration: $F = ma$
- Acceleration = force ÷ mass : $a = \dfrac{F}{m}$
- Mass expressed in kilograms: kg
- Acceleration expressed in meters per second squared: m/s^2
- Force expressed in newtons: N

HESI Tip: Weight is equal to mass times gravitational force. We know the gravitational quotient is 9.8 m/s². The equation is $w = mg$. If we know the mass of an object, it is easy to calculate the weight. Remember to be careful using the metric system. If a question provides mass in grams, the unit must be changed to kilograms.

Third Law of Motion

For every action there is an equal and opposite reaction. If an object pushes or pulls another object, that object will also react with an equal force of pushing or pulling.

Friction

Friction is a force that causes objects in motion to slow down. Friction opposes the motion.

- Expressed in newtons
- Static friction: Acceleration and friction are balanced (no movement of object)
- Kinetic friction: Acceleration is greater than friction (movement of object)
- Rolling friction: Friction on movement of a wheel

$$\text{net force} = \text{force (acceleration)} + \text{force (friction)}$$

Rotation

Objects do not always move in a straight linear fashion. At times, objects can have motion in a rotating manner. A common reflection of this type of motion is displayed by how many rotations the object makes in any given period of time. For example, rotations per minute (RPMs) is a common measurement when dealing with vehicles and engines.

Angular Speed of Circular Motion

angular displacement = θ	arc length = s
radius = r	angular speed = ω

$$\text{angular displacement} = \frac{\text{arc length}}{\text{radius}}, \text{ or } \theta = \frac{s}{r}$$

$$\text{angular speed} = \frac{\text{angular displacement}}{\text{change in time}}, \text{ or } \omega = \frac{\theta}{\Delta t}$$

HESI Tip: A full rotation of a circle contains 2π radians. A radian is a unit that describes angles. One radian has an angle that equals the length of the radius.

Acceleration of Circular Motion

- Gaining or losing speed
- Angular acceleration (α)

$$\alpha = \frac{\Delta \omega}{\Delta t}$$

HESI Tip: Remember, a change in something is reflected symbolically as "Δ."

Uniform Circular Motion

Objects in circular motion can experience what is called a centripetal acceleration. Centripetal acceleration is a rotational motion and a type of acceleration. Although the object does not change speed, because acceleration is a vector quantity of velocity over time, the direction may be changing, thus affecting acceleration. An example of circular motion is a tornado or hurricane. The farther out from the center or core, the faster the circular motion and, in turn, the greater the circular force. There are a variety of factors present in many centripetal forces; in the case of a tornado, it is pressure gradients. The full concept is complicated, but for the HESI A2, a general understanding, including the calculations below, is sufficient.

Centripetal Acceleration

centripetal acceleration = a_c	speed of object = v (m/s)	radius of circle = r

$$a_c = \frac{v^2}{r}$$

Centripetal Force

- Exists alongside centripetal acceleration

centripetal force = F_c	mass of object = m
velocity = v	radius of circle = r

$$F_c = \frac{mv^2}{r}$$

HESI Tip: You may need to rearrange the equation to solve for the desired value. For example, you may be asked to solve for velocity. In this case, you would need to utilize algebra to rework the equation to $v = \sqrt{\frac{F_c r}{m}}$. If you are rusty on moving values around in algebra, it would be a good idea to practice now. Much of physics may call for you to use algebra to rearrange a formula.

Kinetic Energy and Potential Energy

When understanding energy in physics for the HESI A2, the most important form is mechanical energy. There are many other types, such as chemical and nuclear; these are not covered here. In physics, energy is defined as the ability for an object to perform work. Remember, energy is neither created nor destroyed. It is merely transferred or stored.

Potential Energy

- Energy in an object for work to come
- Scalar quantity

- Gravitational potential energy (energy by height of object): Weight × height
  - Expressed in joules (also called newton-meters)

gravitational potential energy = GPE	mass = m
height = h	acceleration due to gravity = g

$$GPE = mgh$$

HESI Tip: Remember, gravity is expressed as 9.8 m/s². In the above equation, mass is reflected in kilograms and height is expressed in meters.

Kinetic Energy

- Energy from movement of objects
- Scalar quantity
- Expressed in joules (also called newton-meters)

kinetic energy = KE	mass = m	velocity = v

$$KE = \frac{1}{2}mv^2$$

HESI Tip: Potential energy and kinetic energy are interchangeable through work. Unless friction or air resistance exists, the energy stays potential or kinetic. For example, if friction exists, some energy may be lost in the form of heat.

Linear Momentum and Impulse

Momentum is simply defined as an object in motion. The amount of motion can be measured and is shown by Newton's second law, which states that any change in momentum is proportional to forces that act on it. A conservation exists. An impulse is defined as a change in the momentum of an object when there is an exertion force acted on it over a period of time. An example is how a driver's movement is slowed down by an airbag during an accident. The goal of the impulse of the airbag is to protect the driver from a blunt force.

Momentum

- Vector quantity
- Displayed in kilogram-meters per second

momentum = p	mass = m	velocity = v

- Momentum (p) is mass × change in velocity, or $p = m\Delta v$.
- Conservation: Must be the same before and after events
  - v_1' = initial velocity of object 1
  - v_2' = initial velocity of object 2
  - v_1 = final velocity of object 1
  - v_2 = final velocity of object 2

- Momentum equation:

$$m_1 v_1' + m_2 v_2' = m_1 v_1 + m_2 v_2$$

HESI Tip: In the momentum equation above, you can see the momentum on both sides has to be equal to accomplish conservation. This allows the manipulation of the equation using algebra to solve for any value a question may request. Move the value of interest to one side of the equation and plug in the numbers given.

Impulse

- Vector quantity

impulse = J	force = F	mass = m	velocity = v

- Impulse equation:

$$J = F\Delta t \text{ and } F\Delta t = m\Delta v$$

Universal Gravitation

The law of universal gravitation in Newtonian physics describes how all particles in the universe attract each other with a force proportional to their mass. It is commonly used today when calculating the effect of gravity on objects. It is also often called force of attraction.

- Gravitation constant = G (6.67×10^{-11} Nm^2/kg^2)

force of attraction = F	mass of object 1 = m_1
mass of object 2 = m_2	distance between objects = r

$$F = \frac{Gm_1 m_2}{r^2}$$

Waves: Sound and Light

Sound

Sound is the audible vibration of wavelengths through air (any gas), liquid, or solid. These wavelengths cause a change in pressure that can be perceived by the human ear. There are many applications outside of physiology, but as healthcare professionals, this is a common understanding of the mechanical wave called sound.

Waves

- Wavelength: Distance between waves
- Frequency: Number of waves in time (hertz)
- Amplitude: Size of the wave vertically

frequency = f	period = T

$$f = \frac{1}{T}$$

HESI Tip: The above equation shows the inverse relationship between frequency and period of the wave.

Mechanical Waves

- Wave through air, liquid, or solid (medium)
- Mechanical movement of the medium
- Example: Earthquake (seismic)
- Example: Sound (audible tones)
  - Ultrasound diagnostics

Electromagnetic Waves

- Electric or magnetic
- Example: Visible light
- Example: X-rays

HESI Tip: Mechanical waves travel at varying speeds, whereas electromagnetic waves travel at the speed of light. Electromagnetic waves are not hindered by a medium such as water; they travel through space.

Speed of Waves

frequency = f	wavelength = λ	velocity = v

$$v = f\lambda$$

Light Waves

- Speed of light = 3.0×10^8 meters per second
- Light is energy, absorbed by materials (electrons).
- Reflection
  - Incident wave: Strikes the mirror
  - Reflected wave: Bounces off
- Refraction
  - Bending of light waves
  - Level of refraction based on medium
    - Slow medium: Light refracts toward the normal
    - Fast medium: Light refracts away from the normal
  - Convex lens: Positive focal length
  - Concave lens: Negative focal length
  - Snell's law ($n_1 \sin\theta_1 = n_2 \sin\theta_2$)
- Index of refraction

index of refraction = n	speed of light = c	speed of light in medium = v_s

$$n = \frac{c}{v_s}$$

HESI Tip: A good example of reflected/refracted light physiologically is eyesight. People who have myopia (nearsightedness) or hyperopia (farsightedness) have alterations to the lens, causing light to be refracted improperly. Snell's law applies to optical devices, such as fiber optics.

Electricity

Charged particles such as protons and electrons form the phenomenon known as electricity. Since its discovery, electricity has been applied to numerous technologies. Natural phenomena also occur, such as lightning. On the atomic level, protons cause positive charges, and electrons cause negative charges. Specifically, valence electrons (outermost shell) determine conductivity.

Coulomb's Law

- Magnitude of force (F) between two charged particles
- Scalar quantity (amount of electrical force)
- Opposite charges attract; identically charged particles repel
- Coulomb's constant = 9×10^9 N-m^2/C^2

charge of object 1 = q_1	charge of object 2 = q_2
Coulomb's constant = k	distance between objects = r

$$F = \frac{kq_1q_2}{r^2}$$

Current

- Movement of electron particles
- Measured in amperes (A)
- The speed-charged particles flow through a conducted medium.

Electric Fields

- Vector quantity

magnitude of electric field = E	force of test charge = F	magnitude of test charge = q_0

$$E = \frac{F}{q_0}$$

Voltage

- Measured in volts (V)
- Potential energy of electricity
- Calculate volts (V) with power (P) in watts and amperes (C or A)

$$V = \frac{P}{C}$$

Resistance

- Measured in ohms (Ω)
- Slowing of electrical currents

Circuits

- Electrical charges flow from positive to negative ends.
- Series circuits: One pathway of current
- Parallel circuits: Multiple pathways of current
- Ohm's law
  - Voltage and resistance affect circuit currents.

voltage = V (volts)	current = I (amperes)	resistance = R (ohms)

$$V = IR$$

Magnetism and Electricity

When electricity moves as a current, a magnetic field is created. The magnetic field in space is called a flux. Elliptical loops of magnetic flux exist in many circumstances. For example, there is one around Earth—it determines how a compass operates. Other examples are diagnostic imaging machines such as x-ray, CT, and MRI.

Electromagnetism

- Tesla: Strength of magnetic flux
- Moving electricity causes magnetism.
- Moving magnetism causes electricity.
- Opposite poles attract.
- Same poles repel.

HESI Tip: Conductors are materials that "conduct" electricity well. Examples are iron and copper, both very common materials used in relation to electricity. Magnetism refers to the attraction of, specifically, iron, cobalt, and nickel.

Practice Quiz

1. A boat moves across a lake for 15 minutes. At the end of the trip, the boat has traveled 5 kilometers. What is the average speed of the boat?

   A. 1.1 m/s
   B. 1.3 m/s
   C. 5.6 m/s
   D. 55 m/s

2. At the beginning of a sprint run for the Olympics, a runner begins the race in a straight line down the track at a consistent speed of 1 m/s^2. What is the speed of the runner after 15 seconds of the race?

   A. 1 m/s
   B. 10 m/s
   C. 15 m/s
   D. 30 m/s

3. A ball thrown down a street has an initial speed of 30 m/s. The ball travels for 30 seconds. What is the acceleration of the ball if the speed at 15 seconds is 60 m/s?

   A. 1.0 m/s^2
   B. 2.0 m/s^2
   C. 4.0 m/s^2
   D. 15 m/s^2

4. A diver falls off of a diving board toward a pool. The diving board is 30 m tall. If the human's horizontal speed is 2.0 m/s, how far out will the diver land in the pool? No air resistance is assumed. Round your answer to the nearest tenth.

   A. 2.5 m
   B. 4.0 m
   C. 5.0 m
   D. 6.1 m

5. A cart is sitting in the street being pushed on opposite sides by two people. The person on the right side is pushing with 20 N of force. The person on the left side is pushing with 30 N of force. If the cart weighs 100 kg, what is the magnitude of the acceleration? Assume there is no friction between the cart and the road.

   A. 0.1 m/s^2
   B. 1.0 m/s^2
   C. 10 m/s^2
   D. 50 m/s^2

6. A ball on the end of a string is spinning around a center point. The radius of the ball to the center is 2 meters. It takes the ball 10 seconds to complete a full rotation. What is the linear speed of the ball? Round to one decimal place.

   A.   0.4 m/s
   B.   0.8 m/s
   C.   1 m/s
   D.   1.3 m/s

7. A cat has a weight of 75 N. What is the mass of the cat?

   A.   7.65 g
   B.   75 g
   C.   7500 g
   D.   7650 g

8. A group of workers are pushing and pulling a large brick of limestone on the ground toward a pyramid. The net force being applied to the brick is 12,000 N. As the brick slides toward the pyramid, it experiences friction from the ground at a magnitude of 800 N. What is the net force acting on the brick?

   A.   12,800 N
   B.   12,000 N
   C.   11,200 N
   D.   200 N

9. A wheel on a car speeds up to 20 revolutions per second from 5 revolutions per second. It takes 10 seconds to achieve this change. What is the angular acceleration of the wheel?

   A.   1.5 revolutions/s^2
   B.   3 revolutions/s^2
   C.   15 revolutions/s^2
   D.   100 revolutions/s^2

10. Kids in an elementary school are playing tetherball. The 0.5-kg ball has been struck and begins moving at a speed of 9 m/s. The rope holding the ball is 4 meters long. Before the ball is struck in the opposite direction, what was the centripetal force and tension of the rope? Round to the nearest whole number.

    A.   2 N
    B.   10 N
    C.   16 N
    D.   18 N

11. A medicine ball is being held over a balcony on a two-story building. The current height of the ball from the ground is 9 meters. The ball weighs 10 N. What is the potential energy of the ball?

    A. 9.8 J
    B. 90 J
    C. 882 J
    D. 980 J

12. A volleyball weighing 2.6 kg travels over a net at a speed of 1 m/s. A player spikes the ball back over the net at a speed of 10 m/s. What impulse affected the volleyball?

    A. 10 N
    B. 9 N
    C. 2.6 N
    D. 23 N

13. Object 1 is placed 100 meters from Object 2. Object 1 has a mass of 1000 kg. Object 2 has a mass of 5000 kg. What is the force between these two objects?

    A. 3.34×10^{-3}
    B. 3.34×10^{-4} N
    C. 3.34×10^{-8} N
    D. 6.67×10^{-11} N

14. When played, a string on a violin emits a note at 440 Hz with a wavelength of 0.773 m. This note is called A. What is the speed of travel for this note on the violin?

    A. 220 m/s
    B. 340 m/s
    C. 440 m/s
    D. 500 m/s

15. While observing light from air penetrate into water, the light refracts. If the light ray approached the water at a 44-degree angle and the same light ray through water was observed at a 33-degree angle, what is the index of refraction for water?

    A. 1.65
    B. 1.33
    C. 1.00
    D. 0.53

16. While rubbing a balloon on a wool sweater, the balloon obtains a charge of 2 C. That balloon is then placed 0.5 meter away from another object with a charge of 10 C. What is the force between the balloon and the second object?

    A. 72 N
    B. 80 N
    C. 3.6×10^{11} N
    D. 7.2×10^{11} N

17. A 500-V power supply is sent through a 75-ohm resistor and a 25-ohm resistor; the resistors are side by side. What is the current flowing through this circuit?

    A.   5 amp
    B.   10 amp
    C.   100 amp
    D.   400 amp

18. What is the momentum of a 100-kg boulder rolling at 10 m/s?

    A.   1000 m/s
    B.   1000 kg m/s
    C.   90 kg m/s
    D.   10 kg m/s

19. A 1000-kg car is driving down a highway at a speed of 72 km/h. What is the kinetic energy of the car?

    A.   2,592,000 J
    B.   200,000 J
    C.   72,000 J
    D.   10,000 J

20. A sound wave cycles 10 times in 20 seconds. What is the period of the sound wave?

    A.   0.5 s
    B.   2 s
    C.   100 s
    D.   200 s

21. What is the difference between insulators and conductors?

    A.   Insulators speed up electrons; conductors do not.
    B.   Insulators stop electrons; conductors allow electrons to pass.
    C.   Conductors allow electrons to pass; insulators slow electrons down.
    D.   Resistors speed up electrons; insulators do not.

22. A refrigerator typically uses 725 watts of power according to the United States Department of Energy. If the refrigerator draws 6 amperes, how many volts is the appliance?

    A.   100 volts
    B.   108 volts
    C.   120 volts
    D.   4,350 volts

23. A taxicab in New York City takes a passenger from the passenger's home to work. The next day, the passenger takes a taxi from home again; however, due to traffic, a different route is taken to the same office. Which of the following statements is true?

    A. The displacement for the first trip is larger.
    B. The displacement for the second trip is larger.
    C. The displacement for both trips is different.
    D. The displacement for both trips is the same.

24. The train on a rollercoaster travels through a loop at 50 km/h. If the diameter of the loop is 20 meters, what is the acceleration of the train?

    A. 2.5 m/s^2
    B. 9.6 m/s^2
    C. 14 m/s^2
    D. 19 m/s^2

25. A small rocket is sent into the air at a speed of 100 m/s. What would the vertical velocity of the rocket be after 5 seconds, assuming the speed is constant?

    A. −41 m/s
    B. 25 m/s
    C. 51 m/s
    D. 95 m/s

Answer Explanations

1. **C.** Start by changing minutes into seconds. Remember to pay close attention to the units of the answers. It is also necessary in this question to change kilometers into meters, an easy conversion in this case. Next utilize the equation for average speed. Average speed equals distance divided by time.

$$\text{average speed} = \frac{\text{distance}}{\text{time}}$$
$$= \frac{5 \text{ km}}{15 \text{ minutes}}$$
$$= \frac{5{,}000 \text{ m}}{900 \text{ seconds}}$$
$$= 5.555 \text{ m/s}$$
$$\approx 5.6 \text{ m/s, choice C}$$

2. **C.** This question is describing the velocity of the runner. The equation for velocity with a constant acceleration is $v = v_0 + at$. The runner begins the race at a zero velocity $v_0 = 0$. In addition, $v = (1 \text{ m/s}^2)(15 \text{ s}) = 15 \text{ m/s}$, choice C. A tricky part of physics questions can sometimes be which terminology the question is trying to describe. For a question like this, the first step is to acknowledge that the term here is "acceleration." Once the term is understood, the appropriate equation can be used.

3. **B.** The equation for acceleration is $a = \frac{v_f - v_i}{\Delta t}$. Putting in the information provided in the question derives the answer.

$$a = \frac{v_f - v_i}{\Delta t}$$
$$= \frac{60 - 30}{15}$$
$$= 2.0 \text{ m/s}^2, \text{ choice B}$$

A question like this is fairly straightforward. It may become more complicated if you were asked to solve for the change in time or other components of the equation. Remember to utilize algebra and move the equation around to solve for what the question is asking.

4. **C.** The diver fell off the board, so the vertical acceleration is zero. The gravitational constant is 9.8. First, solve for time of flight. The equation $d = \frac{1}{2}at^2$ can be reworked to form $t = \sqrt{\frac{2d}{a}}$. Once the numbers are applied and solved, time of flight is found to be 2.5 seconds.

$$t = \sqrt{\frac{2d}{a}}$$
$$= \sqrt{\frac{(2)(30)}{(9.8)}}$$
$$\approx \sqrt{6.1}$$
$$\approx 2.5 \text{ seconds}$$

The horizontal distance equation is $d_x = v_x t$. Using this equation, the distance the diver has traveled can be found. This question assumes there is no air resistance and that the diver did not jump vertically before falling to the pool.

$$d_x = v_x \times t$$
$$= 2 \times 2.5$$
$$= 5 \text{ m}$$

The diver will land 5 meters out, choice C.

5. **A.** First, calculate the net force from both sides of the cart. Net force = $F_{left} + (-) F_{right}$. The net force in this case calculates to 10 N of force to the right.

$$\text{net force} = 30 - 20$$
$$= 10 \text{ N}$$

Taking the net force, apply Newton's second law equation $F = ma$. We are solving for magnitude of acceleration, so rework the equation to solve for a: $a = \dfrac{F}{m}$.

$$a = \frac{F}{m}$$
$$= \frac{10}{100}$$
$$= 0.1 \text{ m/s}^2, \text{ choice A}$$

6. **D.** Start by finding the circumference. The question gives you the radius; the formula for circumference is 2 times the radius pi or $2\pi r$. Substituting 3.14 for π, the circumference is 12.6 meters.

$$2\pi r = (2)(3.14)(2)$$
$$= 12.56$$
$$\approx 12.6 \text{ m}$$

That is the distance the ball must travel to perform a full rotation. To find the speed of an object, the equation is speed $= \dfrac{\text{distance}}{\text{time}}$. Plug in the numbers to solve the problem.

$$\text{speed} = \frac{\text{distance}}{\text{time}}$$
$$= \frac{12.6}{10}$$
$$= 1.26 \text{ m/s}$$
$$\approx 1.3 \text{ m/s}, \text{ choice D}$$

7. **D.** The equation for weight is $w = mg$. This question is asking you to solve for mass and the weight is provided. Rework the equation to solve for m: $m = \dfrac{w}{g}$. Remember the gravitational quotient is 9.8 m/s².

$$m = \frac{w}{g}$$
$$= \frac{75}{9.8}$$
$$\approx 7.65$$

You're not done yet. The answer above is in kilograms, but the answer choices are in grams. You must convert to grams: 7.65 kg = 7650 g, choice D.

8. **C.** There are many theories on how ancient Egyptians built the pyramids, but one obstacle that they had to overcome was the friction and physics of the massive project. Net force is simply the summation of all forces acting on an object. Since the workers are pushing and pulling in the same direction, those forces are not opposing each other. The opposing force here is the friction of 800 N. By subtracting the opposing friction from the net force, the correct answer is found.

$$12,000 \text{ N} - 800 \text{ N} = 11,200 \text{ N, choice C}$$

9. **A.** The formula for angular acceleration, α, is the equation $\alpha = \dfrac{\Delta \omega}{\Delta t}$. All of the information required is provided in the question. The change in revolutions comes to 15. Dividing the change in revolutions by the time of 10 seconds provided brings the correct answer.

$$\text{angular acceleration} = \frac{\Delta \omega}{\Delta t}$$
$$= \frac{20 - 5}{10}$$
$$= \frac{15}{10}$$
$$= 1.5 \text{ revolutions/s}^2, \text{ choice A}$$

10. **B.** The centripetal force formula is $F_c = \dfrac{mv^2}{r}$. The radius in this equation is the length of the rope to the ball. When the ball makes a full rotation, that would be a circle.

$$F_c = \frac{mv^2}{r}$$
$$= \frac{(0.5)(9)^2}{4}$$
$$= 10.125$$
$$\approx 10 \text{ N, choice B}$$

It is important to remember that these equations may need to be reworked to solve for different answers. A similar question may ask you to solve for speed rather than tension.

11. **C.** Potential energy may be stored in many different ways. An archer pulling back a bow string, a compressed coil, human hands before they clap—these are all examples of potential energy. This question is eliciting gravitational potential energy. The equation for this is $PE = mgh$.

$$PE = mgh$$
$$= (10)(9.8)(9)$$
$$= 882 \text{ J, choice C}$$

12. **D.** Impulse is defined as the change in momentum of an object. Momentum is simply any object in motion. It can be easy to confuse the terms since they are so closely related. This question is talking about impulse, or rather, the change in speed of the volleyball when it is hit back. The equation to find the impulse is $p = m\Delta v$.

$$p = m\Delta v$$
$$= 2.6(10.0 - 1.0)$$
$$= (2.6)(9.0)$$
$$= 23.4$$
$$\approx 23 \text{ N, choice D}$$

13. **C.** This question might be inherently tricky for some people due to multiplying exponents and scientific notation. Do not let this confuse you. The equation for universal gravitation is $F = \dfrac{Gm_1m_2}{r^2}$. Using this equation, solve for F.

$$F = \frac{Gm_1m_2}{r^2}$$
$$= \frac{(6.67 \times 10^{-11} \text{ Nm}^2/\text{kg}^2)(1,000)(5,000)}{100^2}$$
$$= \frac{(6.67 \times 10^{-5} \text{ Nm}^2/\text{kg}^2)(5)}{100^2}$$
$$= \frac{(33.35 \times 10^{-5} \text{ Nm}^2/\text{kg}^2)}{100^2}$$
$$= \frac{(33.35 \times 10^{-5} \text{ Nm}^2/\text{kg}^2)}{10,000}$$
$$= 33.35 \times 10^{-9}$$
$$= 3.335 \times 10^{-8}$$
$$\approx 3.34 \times 10^{-8}, \text{ choice C}$$

14. **B.** This question is fairly straightforward using the proper equation, speed $= f\lambda$. Remember, the lambda symbol reflects the wavelength. As a reference, the human ear can typically hear between 20 Hz to 2,000 Hz.

$$\text{speed} = f\lambda$$
$$= (440)(0.773)$$
$$= 340.12$$
$$\approx 340 \text{ m/s, choice B}$$

15. **B.** Snell's law is used to find the answer to this question; $n_1 \sin\theta_1 = n_2 \sin\theta_2$. Since n_1 is refraction of air, a number that is, for all intents and purposes, 1, it becomes easier to rework the equation to solve for the answer being asked. Rework the equation to solve for n_2. The degrees are given in the question.

$$n_1 \sin\theta_1 = n_2 \sin\theta_2$$
$$1 \sin 44 = n_2 \sin 33$$
$$\frac{\sin 44}{\sin 33} = n_2$$
$$1.33... = n_2$$
$$1.33 \approx n_2, \text{ choice B}$$

16. **D.** Utilize Coulomb's law to answer this question: $F = \dfrac{kq_1q_2}{r^2}$. All of the needed information is presented in the question. Remember that k equals a constant (9×10^9 N-m^2/C^2).

$$F = \frac{kq_1q_2}{r^2}$$
$$= \frac{(9\times10^9\,\text{N})(2)(10)}{0.5^2}$$
$$= \frac{18\times10^{10}}{0.25}$$
$$= 72\times10^{10}\,\text{N}$$
$$= 7.2\times10^{11}\,\text{N, choice D}$$

17. **A.** Ohm's law equation is used to solve this problem. The equation $V = IR$ can be changed to solve for I. That equation is $I = \dfrac{V}{R}$. The total resistance is found by adding the individual resistor ohms, totaling 100 ohms.

$$I = \frac{V}{R}$$
$$= \frac{500}{75+25}$$
$$= \frac{500}{100}$$
$$= 5 \text{ amp, choice A}$$

18. **B.** Momentum is found by multiplying mass and velocity. If there were a change in the velocity, it would be the change itself that would be multiplied by mass. In this case, the question does not display a change in the boulder's speed; it is a consistent 10 m/s. The equation is $p = mv$ or $p = m\Delta v$.

$$p = mv$$
$$= (100)(10)$$
$$= 1000 \text{ kg m/s, choice B}$$

19. **B.** Kinetic energy is affected by the velocity of the car and the mass of the car. The equation $KE = \frac{1}{2}mv^2$ is used. Remember to change 72 km/hr into m/s. The unit must be in meters per second, not kilometers per hour. 1 Joule = 1 kg m²s².

$$KE = \frac{1}{2}mv^2$$
$$= \frac{1}{2}(1,000)(72)^2$$
$$= \frac{1}{2}(1,000)(20.0000016)^2$$
$$= \frac{1}{2}(20,000.0016)^2$$
$$= \frac{1}{2}(400,000,064)$$
$$= 200,000,032$$
$$\approx 200,000 \text{ J, choice B}$$

20. **B.** A wave period describes the amount of time for one cycle to complete the wave. If this sound wave cycles 10 times in 20 seconds, simply divide 20 by 10. The period of the sound wave is 2 s, choice B.

21. **C.** "To conduct" describes the conveying or transmitting of something. In this sense, it is electricity or electrons. A conductor aids in the movement of electrons. A good example would be copper or aluminum. Insulators slow down the movement of electrons. Therefore, choice C is correct: Conductors allow electrons to pass; insulators slow electrons down.

22. **C.** The equation for power is fairly simple: power (watts) = volts × current. This can be reworked to solve for voltage: $V = \frac{P}{C}$.

$$V = \frac{P}{C}$$
$$= \frac{725}{6}$$
$$= 120.833...$$
$$\approx 120 \text{ volts, choice C}$$

23. **D.** Do not confuse distance and displacement. The distance for the second trip is likely longer due to the traffic, but the displacement is the same. The starting position and the final position for both trips is the same, ergo the displacement is the same, choice D.

24. **D.** First, kilometers per hour needs to be changed to meters per second to match the format of the answer choices. This question is asking for the centripetal acceleration of the train as it travels through the loop at 50 km/h = 13.88889 m/s. The equation used is $a_c = \dfrac{v^2}{r}$. Remember that a radius is half of the diameter.

$$a_c = \frac{v^2}{r}$$
$$= \frac{13.88889^2}{10}$$
$$\approx \frac{192.90}{10}$$
$$\approx 19.29$$
$$\approx 19 \text{ m/s}^2, \text{ choice D}$$

25. **C.** None of the values need to be converted, so simply input the values into the equation $v_f = v_i - (g \times t)$.

$$v_f = v_i - (g \times t)$$
$$= 100 - (9.8 \times 5)$$
$$= 100 - 49$$
$$= 51 \text{ m/s, choice C}$$

Vertical velocity must be great enough to escape gravity, a problem the people at NASA know quite well. This rocket is fairly small, so eventually it would succumb to gravity and the result would be a negative velocity.

Chapter 9

Biology Practice Exam

At 25 questions, this practice exam reflects the length of the biology section on the HESI A2. Do not concern yourself with time for the purpose of this exercise. While the HESI itself is typically timed at 25 minutes per section, a well-prepared student will rarely run out of time.

The goal of this practice exam is to achieve a score of 70%–80% or higher. While students who perform below this level often do fine on the HESI A2, it is a benchmark to keep in mind if additional study and questions would help overall preparation. Good luck, future nurses and providers! Take a deep breath and begin.

Answer Sheet

1 Ⓐ Ⓑ Ⓒ Ⓓ
2 Ⓐ Ⓑ Ⓒ Ⓓ
3 Ⓐ Ⓑ Ⓒ Ⓓ
4 Ⓐ Ⓑ Ⓒ Ⓓ
5 Ⓐ Ⓑ Ⓒ Ⓓ

6 Ⓐ Ⓑ Ⓒ Ⓓ
7 Ⓐ Ⓑ Ⓒ Ⓓ
8 Ⓐ Ⓑ Ⓒ Ⓓ
9 Ⓐ Ⓑ Ⓒ Ⓓ
10 Ⓐ Ⓑ Ⓒ Ⓓ

11 Ⓐ Ⓑ Ⓒ Ⓓ
12 Ⓐ Ⓑ Ⓒ Ⓓ
13 Ⓐ Ⓑ Ⓒ Ⓓ
14 Ⓐ Ⓑ Ⓒ Ⓓ
15 Ⓐ Ⓑ Ⓒ Ⓓ

16 Ⓐ Ⓑ Ⓒ Ⓓ
17 Ⓐ Ⓑ Ⓒ Ⓓ
18 Ⓐ Ⓑ Ⓒ Ⓓ
19 Ⓐ Ⓑ Ⓒ Ⓓ
20 Ⓐ Ⓑ Ⓒ Ⓓ

21 Ⓐ Ⓑ Ⓒ Ⓓ
22 Ⓐ Ⓑ Ⓒ Ⓓ
23 Ⓐ Ⓑ Ⓒ Ⓓ
24 Ⓐ Ⓑ Ⓒ Ⓓ
25 Ⓐ Ⓑ Ⓒ Ⓓ

25 Questions

Directions: Each of the following questions is followed by four answer choices. Choose the one best answer, marking it on the answer sheet provided.

1. In genetics, many diseases have been mapped on the genome and their origins, therefore, are understood. When discussing the genetics of parents or individuals, what do the terms *heterozygous* and *homozygous* represent?

    A. Dominant alleles
    B. Phenotype
    C. Mutations
    D. Allele combinations

2. What is the main feature of a eukaryotic organism?

    A. Eukaryotic organisms contain a nucleus that holds DNA.
    B. Eukaryotic organisms do not have a nucleus.
    C. Eukaryotic organisms are the simplest form of organism.
    D. Eukaryotic organisms are bacteria.

3. Which of the following classifications is the most specific and includes the least organisms?

    A. Genus
    B. Order
    C. Species
    D. Family

4. Which of the following describes a condensation reaction?

    A. The reaction releases water.
    B. The reaction absorbs water.
    C. The reaction occurs most frequently with carbohydrates.
    D. The reaction occurs most frequently with lipids.

5. What is the difference between rough and smooth endoplasmic reticulum (ER) inside of a cell?

    A. Smooth ER does not have vacuoles attached.
    B. Smooth ER does not have ribosomes attached.
    C. Rough ER commonly breaks down molecules.
    D. Smooth ER commonly builds proteins.

6. The citric acid cycle (Krebs cycle) is crucial for the creation of energy for many organisms. Which of the following compounds is created by glycolysis and utilized in the citric acid cycle?

   A. Adenosine diphosphate (ADP)
   B. Oxygen
   C. Lactic acid
   D. Pyruvate

7. During apoptosis or cell death, the cell membrane is destroyed. What is the primary component that makes up a cell membrane?

   A. Amino acids
   B. Carbohydrates
   C. Lipids
   D. Proteins

8. What is the name of the molecule that gives plants their green color and is essential in photosynthesis?

   A. Cyanobacteria
   B. Chlorophyll
   C. Chloroplast
   D. Carotenoid

9. Which of the following is the correct order for the scientific method?

   A. Identify a problem, form a hypothesis, evaluate and form conclusions, perform experiments, observe results
   B. Evaluate and form conclusions, identify a problem, observe results, perform experiments, form a hypothesis
   C. Form a hypothesis, perform experiments, identify a problem, observe results, evaluate and form conclusions
   D. Identify a problem, form a hypothesis, perform experiments, observe results, evaluate and form conclusions

10. Which of the following is an accurate description for the polarity of water?

    A. Water has a negative charge on the oxygen atom and positive charges on the hydrogen atoms.
    B. The polarity of water makes it difficult for other compounds to dissolve in it.
    C. The polarity of water makes it repel other water molecules.
    D. Water is highly polar, which makes it difficult for it to move between membranes.

11. The common pet dog has 78 chromosomes in its diploid cells. What would the haploid number of chromosomes be for a dog's gametes?

    A. 39
    B. 48
    C. 78
    D. 156

12. The term *organic* means matter that is living or alive, a common study in biology and chemistry. In organic matter, which of the following elements best describes *organic*?

    A. Carbon
    B. Oxygen
    C. Water
    D. Nitrogen

13. Enzymes are crucial to human physiology and survival. What type of macromolecules are enzymes?

    A. Carbohydrates
    B. Proteins
    C. Lipids
    D. Nucleic acids

14. The human body requires a constant replenishment of new cells to continue operating. In the skin, for example, old cells slough off and new cells are created. Which of the following processes reflects this new cell growth?

    A. Mitosis
    B. Meiosis
    C. Binary fission
    D. Sexual reproduction

15. Proteins, being one of the macromolecules, are created often by protein synthesis. Which of the following correctly orders how this process occurs?

    A. Ribosomes → DNA transcription → tRNA → mRNA → amino acids build proteins
    B. Ribosomes → DNA transcription → mRNA → tRNA → amino acids build proteins
    C. DNA transcription → tRNA → ribosomes → mRNA → amino acids build proteins
    D. DNA transcription → mRNA → ribosomes → tRNA → amino acids build proteins

16. A bodybuilder requires strong muscles and energy to lift weights. Which organelle would be required in high amounts in the muscle cells for this athlete to perform?

    A. Mitochondria
    B. Ribosomes
    C. Vacuoles
    D. Endoplasmic reticulum

17. Deoxyribonucleic acid, or simply DNA, holds all of the information within our body. It is a double helix structure that matches nitrogenous bases together. Which of the following base combinations is correct in DNA?

    A. Adenine/cytosine : thymine/guanine
    B. Adenine/thymine : guanine/cytosine
    C. Adenine/uracil : guanine/cytosine
    D. Adenine/thymine : guanine/uracil

18. A catabolic reaction of proteins would create which of the following molecules?

    A. Glycerides
    B. Fatty acids
    C. Glucose
    D. Amino acids

19. Which of the following describes the creation of ATP in the absence of oxygen?

    A. Aerobic respiration
    B. Krebs cycle
    C. Fermentation
    D. Metabolism

20. Which of the following does the classification *Homo sapiens* reflect in the full system of categories?

    A. Genus and species
    B. Kingdom and species
    C. Family and genus
    D. Kingdom and phylum

21. Lipids (fats) contain long chains of fatty acids that can be saturated or unsaturated. What is the correct description of a saturated fatty acid chain?

    A. Linear with multiple double bonds
    B. Linear with no double bonds
    C. Linear and liquid
    D. Nonlinear and liquid

22. Two parents have recently visited a genetic counselor and both were found to be heterozygous for a disease they may pass on to a future child. Which of the following allele combinations reflects a heterozygous allele?

    A. *hH*
    B. *HH*
    C. *Hh*
    D. *hh*

23. Natural selection was first proposed by Charles Darwin in 1859. Which of the following best explains natural selection?

    A. Natural selection is the rapid change and mutation of a species that leads to survival.
    B. Genetics and DNA rarely change; therefore, similar DNA is passed down to offspring.
    C. Mutations are rare; therefore, the success of a species is random.
    D. Certain traits of organisms favor survival; therefore, genetics are passed down to offspring.

24. If a father is heterozygous for a trait (*Hh*) and the mother is homozygous recessive for a trait (*hh*), what is the probability that their child would be homozygous recessive?

    A. 100%
    B. 50%
    C. 25%
    D. 0%

25. Certain lipids form molecules that send signals within the human body. Which of the following is an example of a steroid, a signaling molecule that carries messages to target cells by way of the bloodstream?

    A. Cortisol
    B. Amylase
    C. Bile
    D. ATP

Answer Key

1. D	6. D	11. A	16. A	21. B
2. A	7. C	12. A	17. B	22. C
3. C	8. B	13. B	18. D	23. D
4. A	9. D	14. A	19. C	24. B
5. B	10. A	15. D	20. A	25. A

Answer Explanations

1. **D.** The terms heterozygous and homozygous describe allele combinations, choice D. Heterozygous means the alleles are different: *Hh*. Homozygous means the alleles are the same: *hh* or *HH*. Different traits have different expressions. A trait or allele can be dominant or recessive, but it cannot be assumed to be automatically dominant (choice A) without information. A phenotype (choice B) is the outward expression of a trait, such as hair color or height. Heterozygous and homozygous do not mean mutated genes (choice C). Mutations may occur in DNA through a few different mechanisms, translocation being one of them.

2. **A.** The hallmark feature of eukaryotic organisms is the presence of a nucleus, choice A. Examples would be plants and animals. These organisms are generally complex, not simple (choice C) and do not include bacteria, eliminating choice D.

3. **C.** The classification of life is as follows:

$$\text{kingdom} \rightarrow \text{phylum} \rightarrow \text{class} \rightarrow \text{order} \rightarrow \text{family} \rightarrow \text{genus} \rightarrow \text{species}$$

   Species, choice C, is the most specific.

4. **A.** In a condensation reaction, two molecules are joined in a covalent bond in order to form a larger one. The process also releases the molecule water, choice A, hence condensation. The opposite of a condensation reaction is the hydrolysis reaction, which causes the absorption of water (choice B). The condensation reaction is most commonly seen in the organic molecules, proteins, not carbohydrates (choice C) or lipids (choice D). This reaction is responsible for the creation of large peptides.

5. **B.** The main difference between rough ER and smooth ER is whether or not ribosomes are attached. Ribosomes are not attached in smooth ER, choice B. ER type is associated by ribosomes, not vacuoles, eliminating choice A. Smooth ER, not rough ER, breaks down molecules, eliminating choice C. Rough ER, not smooth ER, builds membranes and proteins, eliminating choice D. In cellular biology, it can be tricky to memorize what every single organelle does, but knowledge of organelles and their functions is important for the HESI A2. Not every question will be easy.

6. **D.** Pyruvate, also called pyruvic acid, is created by glycolysis of glucose and begins the citric acid cycle, choice D. While both oxygen (choice B) and adenosine diphosphate (ADP; choice A) are utilized in the citric acid cycle, they are not created by glycolysis. Lactic acid (choice C) is the byproduct of anaerobic respiration and is commonly used in fermentation by some organisms.

7. **C.** There are three types of lipids, choice C, that make up the cellular membrane: phospholipids, glycolipids, and sterols. Of these, phospholipids make up most of a cell membrane. While proteins (choice D) are present in the cellular membrane, such as integrated proteins for active transport, they do not make up the majority of the membrane itself. Amino acids (choice A) are the monomer, or smaller unit of proteins. The same applies to carbohydrates (choice B); glycolipids exist in the membrane and play an important role in immune function, but are not the majority.

8. **B.** Chlorophyll, choice B, is a green pigment molecule found inside of thylakoids in chloroplasts; it is essential for photosynthesis. Cyanobacteria (choice A) are bacteria, not a molecule. Chloroplasts (choice C) are the plant organelles in which photosynthesis takes place; they are not molecules. Chlorophyll does, however, exist inside chloroplasts. Carotenoids (choice D) are another type of pigment molecule in plants and are essential in photosynthesis, but they are reddish, orange, or yellow hues, not green. This is why carrots are orange; they are high in carotenoids.

9. **D.** The correct order for the scientific method is given in choice D: identify a problem, form a hypothesis, perform experiments, observe results, evaluate and form conclusions.

10. **A.** The word *polar* implies something has "poles" or areas of magnetic or electrical fields. Earth, for example, is polar; that is how a compass works and can point north. The same applies to molecules. Water is polar, with partial positive charges on the hydrogen atom ends, and a partial negative charge in the middle at the oxygen atom, choice A. Water is a great solvent and many things dissolve in it, eliminating choice B. It is also cohesive and sticks to itself very well, eliminating choice C. Water also passes through membranes quite easily, eliminating choice D; this action describes osmosis, an essential action for living things.

11. **A.** A dog's diploid cells contain 78 chromosomes; therefore, its haploid cells, such as gametes, contain half of that—39 chromosomes, choice A. By no means do you need to memorize how many chromosomes organisms have, except for humans, but the terms diploid (two chromosomes per cell) and haploid (one chromosome per cell) should be understood. The other answer choices are not correct for the haploid reflection of 78.

12. **A.** Organic matter describes compounds that are derived from carbon, choice A. Carbon also plays a large part in the study of organic chemistry. Oxygen (choice B) and water (choice C) are both essential for much of the life on this planet, but neither is the backbone of organic matter. Nitrogen (choice D) is found in many things, such as air; however, it is not the main component of organic matter.

13. **B.** Enzymes, such as amylase and lipase used in digestion, are specialized proteins, choice B. Enzymes, like many proteins, are constructed from pieces of amino acids in specific formats. Carbohydrates (choice A), lipids (choice C), and nucleic acids (choice D) do not make up enzymes.

14. **A.** Mitosis is the process within the cell where two identical daughter cells are produced from a parent cell. This process is required for countless body processes, including new cell growth in skin. The skin acts as a barrier to infection; therefore, it is constantly renewed and repaired via mitosis, choice A. Because mitosis requires DNA, it is present only in eukaryotic cells. Prokaryotic cells divide by binary fission (choice C). Sexual reproduction (choice D), the beginnings of which also describe meiosis (choice B), creates haploid, or nonidentical, daughter cells called gametes. These cells are utilized in sperm or eggs.

15. **D.** Protein synthesis can be a difficult topic to master since there are a handful of very important steps. Remember, the information to build the proteins in our body come from the DNA itself. The order of the process is accurately detailed in choice D:

DNA transcription → mRNA → ribosomes → tRNA → amino acids build proteins

Protein synthesis begins with the transcription from DNA to messenger RNA (mRNA). The mRNA then moves to the ribosomes, where the transfer process begins. Codons on the mRNA match an anticodon on the transfer RNA (tRNA). Amino acids exist on the tRNA, and the process of creating the protein begins. The other answer choices do not place the steps of this process in the correct order.

16. **A.** Mitochondria are the powerhouse of a cell. The specific function of a muscle cell would be a discussion within anatomy and physiology; however, from a cellular biology standpoint, an athlete would require many mitochondria, choice A, to perform at a high level. Muscle cells in general have more mitochondria than other cells. The energy requirements of these cells are higher. Ribosomes (choice B) create proteins and can be bound to rough ER (choice D); smooth ER is unbounded. Either way, both organelles create or break down proteins. When thinking about protein as a macromolecule

that we eat, consider the idea of energy. A lot of energy can certainly come from protein, but that requires body metabolism. Do not confuse cellular biology with a larger, or macro, thought. Vacuoles (choice C) transport molecules throughout the cell; they do not influence the energy needs of the human body.

17. **B.** As listed in choice B, the base adenine bonds with thymine, and the base guanine bonds with cytosine. Inside RNA, uracil replaces thymine, so a bond between adenine and uracil would be seen inside RNA. The base combinations in the other answer choices are incorrect.

18. **D.** A catabolic reaction breaks things down. Amino acids are the building blocks of proteins, so a catabolic reaction of proteins would create amino acids, choice D. Glucose (choice C) would be created by a catabolic reaction of a larger sugar, such as a polysaccharide. Fatty acids (choice B) and glycerides (choice A) are components of lipids.

19. **C.** Fermentation, a type of anaerobic respiration, creates ATP without oxygen, choice C. Aerobic respiration (choice A), which includes the Krebs cycle (choice B), requires oxygen to work. Metabolism (choice D) can be tricky to think about. Metabolism as a whole absolutely brings about energy; however, that energy is in the form of breaking down food into smaller components. These components may eventually be used to create ATP, but that does not describe metabolism as a whole.

20. **A.** *Homo sapiens* reflects the genus and the species, choice A, of human beings. You do not need to memorize all life and how it is classified; that would require significant training. However, knowledge of the full taxonomy of human beings is valuable. The way it is presented is also important. Note that the genus *Homo* is capitalized, whereas the species *sapiens* is not. *Canis lupus*, for example, is better known as a dog. Many people are familiar with the word "canis" or "canine," derived from Latin. The classifications listed in the other answer choices are incorrect. The full taxonomy for humans is as follows:

Kingdom	Phylum	Class	Order	Family	Genus	Species
Animalia	*Chordata*	*Vertebrata*	*Mammalia*	*Primate*	*Homoinidae*	*Homo*	*sapiens*

21. **B.** Fatty acids are crucial to proper body function. The only way to get them is through food because the body cannot recreate them. Fatty acid chains are one part of a lipid; the other is the glycerol head. The fatty acid chains themselves have the two names: saturated or unsaturated. A saturated fatty acid has no double bonds, giving it a linear appearance, choice B. Saturated fatty acids also tend to be solid at room temperature. Unsaturated fatty acids are liquid (choices C and D), have one or more double bonds (choice A), and have a nonlinear appearance (choice D), giving them a branching look.

22. **C.** Heterozygous or the word "hetero" more specifically means "other" in Latin, or "different." The correct way to present a heterozygous allele is *Hh*, choice C. While *hH* (choice A) may also appear to present a heterozygous combination, it is not written this way in genetics. The allele combinations *HH* (choice B) and *hh* (choice D) show a homozygous combination since both alleles are the same.

23. **D.** There is a significant amount of diversity within any given species. Over time, a phenotype or outward trait is favorable to survival, such as colorful feathers of birds attracting more mates. More of this species survived due to their ability to increase the amount of offspring. The genetics then continued to pass down as the species reproduced. Natural selection is often referred to as "survival of the fittest." Only the strong survive. Choice D best explains natural selection: Certain traits of organisms favor survival; therefore, genetics are passed down to offspring.

Natural selection and evolution in general are rarely rapid, except potentially in the case of punctuated equilibrium, eliminating choice A. Mutations and changes in DNA are also fairly common, eliminating choices B and C, but usually changes are too small to notice. Success of a species is rarely random. Almost always a cause can be found; whether it was geographical or genetic, a reason typically exists.

24. **B.** To find the probability of an offspring, you can use a Punnett square, as shown below.

	H	h
h	Hh	hh
h	Hh	hh

As indicated above, the chances of the child having an *hh* allele, or homozygous recessive, is 50%, choice B. The chances of the child having a heterozygous allele (*Hh*) is also 50%. There is a 0% chance the child would be homozygous dominant, or *HH*. No combination here would result in a 75% probability.

25. **A.** Cortisol, choice A, is the only steroid in this list. Steroids can also be called hormones, such as testosterone and cortisol. Non-steroid hormones would include things like insulin. A more comprehensive list of hormones and steroids can be found in the anatomy and physiology chapter (Chapter 7). For the purpose of biology, it is more important to understand the building blocks. In this case, a steroid is made from lipids, not proteins. Amylase (choice B) is an enzyme created from proteins and amino acids. Bile (choice C) is not a steroid; however, it does aid in the breakdown and digestion of lipids. Adenosine triphosphate, or ATP for short (choice D), as a molecule is technically a nucleotide given its make-up; it is not a steroid.

At 25 questions, this practice exam reflects the length of the anatomy and physiology section on the HESI A2. Do not concern yourself with time for the purpose of this exercise. While the HESI itself is typically timed at 25 minutes per section, a well-prepared student will rarely run out of time.

The goal of this practice exam is to achieve a score of 70%–80% or higher. While students who perform below this level often do fine on the HESI A2, it is a benchmark to keep in mind if additional study and questions would help overall preparation. Good luck, future nurses and providers! Take a deep breath and begin.

Answer Sheet

1 Ⓐ Ⓑ Ⓒ Ⓓ
2 Ⓐ Ⓑ Ⓒ Ⓓ
3 Ⓐ Ⓑ Ⓒ Ⓓ
4 Ⓐ Ⓑ Ⓒ Ⓓ
5 Ⓐ Ⓑ Ⓒ Ⓓ

6 Ⓐ Ⓑ Ⓒ Ⓓ
7 Ⓐ Ⓑ Ⓒ Ⓓ
8 Ⓐ Ⓑ Ⓒ Ⓓ
9 Ⓐ Ⓑ Ⓒ Ⓓ
10 Ⓐ Ⓑ Ⓒ Ⓓ

11 Ⓐ Ⓑ Ⓒ Ⓓ
12 Ⓐ Ⓑ Ⓒ Ⓓ
13 Ⓐ Ⓑ Ⓒ Ⓓ
14 Ⓐ Ⓑ Ⓒ Ⓓ
15 Ⓐ Ⓑ Ⓒ Ⓓ

16 Ⓐ Ⓑ Ⓒ Ⓓ
17 Ⓐ Ⓑ Ⓒ Ⓓ
18 Ⓐ Ⓑ Ⓒ Ⓓ
19 Ⓐ Ⓑ Ⓒ Ⓓ
20 Ⓐ Ⓑ Ⓒ Ⓓ

21 Ⓐ Ⓑ Ⓒ Ⓓ
22 Ⓐ Ⓑ Ⓒ Ⓓ
23 Ⓐ Ⓑ Ⓒ Ⓓ
24 Ⓐ Ⓑ Ⓒ Ⓓ
25 Ⓐ Ⓑ Ⓒ Ⓓ

25 Questions

Directions: Each of the following questions is followed by four answer choices. Choose the one best answer, marking it on the answer sheet provided.

1. In what area of the vasculature would you expect to find deoxygenated blood?

   A. Aorta
   B. Coronary artery
   C. Pulmonary artery
   D. Arterioles

2. A person who is choking is unable to get air into or out of their lungs. Which structure of the body when occluded causes choking?

   A. Trachea
   B. Esophagus
   C. Alveoli
   D. Diaphragm

3. The brain and the spinal cord make up which portion of the nervous system?

   A. Central nervous system
   B. Peripheral nervous system
   C. Sympathetic nervous system
   D. Parasympathetic nervous system

4. Which of the following specialized tissues cushions and insulates the human body?

   A. Connective tissue
   B. Muscle tissue
   C. Epithelial tissue
   D. Skeletal tissue

5. Which of the following correctly indicates how many directions a hinge joint can move and provides a good example?

   A. One : thumb
   B. Two : elbow
   C. Two : vertebrae
   D. Four : knee

6. Which of the following organs can be said to be superior to the liver?

   A. Kidneys
   B. Brain
   C. Gallbladder
   D. Uterus

7. Which of the following correctly lists the layers of skin from the innermost (deep) to the outermost (superficial) layer?

   A. Dermis, hypodermis, epidermis
   B. Dermis, epidermis, hypodermis
   C. Hypodermis, dermis, epidermis
   D. Epidermis, dermis, hypodermis

8. The striated appearance of skeletal muscle arises from what structural piece?

   A. Myocardium
   B. Endomysium
   C. Sarcomere
   D. Mitochondria

9. If an athlete exercises, resulting in a drop of blood glucose, which hormone would cause the body to correct this issue and increase blood glucose?

   A. Gluconeogenesis
   B. Adrenalin
   C. Insulin
   D. Glucagon

10. Which chamber of the heart is the first area for blood to arrive in the heart from the venous system?

    A. Right atria
    B. Right ventricle
    C. Left atria
    D. Left ventricle

11. When a healthcare provider views an electrocardiogram (ECG/EKG), what are they looking at exactly?

    A. Systolic and diastolic contractions
    B. Electrical activity
    C. Myocardial movement
    D. Receptors in the aorta

12. Which of the following is NOT a part of the alimentary canal?

    A. Liver
    B. Esophagus
    C. Rectum
    D. Jejunum

13. The body can regulate blood pH through a variety of means. Which of the following influences one of these means?

   A.   Carbon dioxide
   B.   Oxygen
   C.   Carbon monoxide
   D.   Nitrogen

14. Filtration of blood through the nephrons of the kidneys occurs due to hydrostatic pressure. What does hydrostatic pressure imply?

   A.   Osmotic pressure
   B.   Blood pressure
   C.   Concentration pressure
   D.   Venous pressure

15. Where in the human body would you expect to find a specialized sudoriferous gland that releases cerumen?

   A.   Skin
   B.   Mouth
   C.   Ears
   D.   Eyes

16. If connective tissue were mineralized with calcium, where would you expect to find this specialized tissue?

   A.   Cartilage
   B.   Bone
   C.   Tendons
   D.   Blood

17. If a person gets injured and begins to bleed, the blood will begin to clot. What type of pathway is clotting, where the clotting itself further increases more clotting?

   A.   Homeostasis
   B.   Variable feedback loop
   C.   Positive feedback loop
   D.   Negative feedback loop

18. Which area of the brain is responsible for heart rate and breathing?

   A.   Medulla oblongata
   B.   Hypothalamus
   C.   Cerebellum
   D.   Cerebrum

19. The thyroid gland is most commonly known to regulate what?

    A. Calcium
    B. Metabolism
    C. Insulin and glucagon
    D. Fight-or-flight response

20. If you place your hand on a hot stove, you feel pain. How would this sensation reach the brain?

    A. Sensory neurons
    B. Motor neurons
    C. Reflex neurons
    D. Association neurons

21. What type of cell develops cartilage?

    A. Osteoblast
    B. Chondrocyte
    C. Erythrocyte
    D. Melanocyte

22. Which of the following is waste products excreted by the kidneys?

    A. Antidiuretic hormone (ADH)
    B. Water and sodium
    C. Bile and ammonia
    D. Creatinine and urea

23. Where does oogenesis occur in the body?

    A. Ovaries
    B. Liver
    C. Pancreas
    D. Brain

24. If a surgeon wanted to dissect an organ into anterior and posterior portions, what type of plane would he cut in?

    A. Horizontal plane
    B. Sagittal plane
    C. Transverse plane
    D. Frontal plane

25. The blood-brain barrier (BBB) protects the brain from unwanted pathogens. How does it do this?

    A. Tight junctions
    B. High blood pressure
    C. Small capillaries
    D. Cerebrospinal fluid

Answer Key

1. C	6. B	11. B	16. B	21. B
2. A	7. C	12. A	17. C	22. D
3. A	8. C	13. A	18. A	23. A
4. A	9. D	14. B	19. B	24. D
5. B	10. A	15. C	20. A	25. A

Answer Explanations

1. **C.** The pulmonary artery, choice C, is the only artery in the body that carries deoxygenated blood. Every other artery, like the aorta (choice A), coronary (choice B), and arterioles (choice D), carries oxygenated blood. Veins typically carry deoxygenated blood, except for the pulmonary vein, which brings oxygenated blood to the left atria of the heart. Make sure to have a good general knowledge of the names of the major arteries and veins. You do not want to slip up on something as simple as a name.

2. **A.** The trachea, commonly known as the windpipe, is the main airway leading down into the bronchi and therefore into the lungs. If the trachea, choice A, is occluded, choking or strangulation will occur. The epiglottis is a commonly talked-about feature in choking. This is the little flap that acts to protect the trachea during swallowing. However, on occasion, something can slip by and cause coughing or, worse, choking. The esophagus (choice B), responsible for swallowing, would not affect a person's ability to breathe in this case. If a piece of food were stuck in the esophagus, a person would still be able to breathe. The alveoli (choice C) are responsible for the exchange of oxygen and carbon dioxide. While they are certainly important in getting oxygen into the bloodstream, they are not a factor in choking. The same is true for the diaphragm (choice D), which is a muscle. The diaphragm is hugely important when breathing, but it does not occlude or cause choking.

3. **A.** The brain and spinal cord make up the anatomical portions of the central nervous system, choice A. The peripheral nervous system (choice B) is everything outside of the brain and spinal cord. With terms like sympathetic (choice C) and parasympathetic (choice D) nervous systems, remember that the term itself does not mean specific areas of the nervous system, but rather a collection or system of control. The terms refer to specific functions of the nervous system. For example, the sympathetic nervous system (choice C), a part of the autonomic nervous system, is involved in the fight-or-flight response.

4. **A.** Adipose tissue is a type of specialized loose connective tissue, choice A, responsible for storing energy, insulating, and protecting the human body. Adipose tissue contains cells called adipocytes that are filled with fat. Muscle tissue (choice B) allows the body to move in many different ways. Epithelial tissue (choice C) lines the skin and organs. Skeletal tissue (choice D) gives the body structure and stores calcium in the form of bones.

5. **B.** A hinge joint can move in two directions. Examples of a hinge joint include the elbow, choice B, as well as the knee, fingers, and toes. The thumb (choice A) is a saddle joint. Vertebrae (choice C) are a type of plane joint, especially in the neck. The knee (choice D) is a hinge joint, but it moves in two directions, not four.

6. **B.** "Superior" means to be above something. In the human body, that literally means toward the head. The only organ listed here that is superior to the liver is the brain, choice B. All of the other organs are inferior to (below) the liver. The gallbladder (choice C) is in close proximity to the liver, but it is still below or inferior to the liver.

7. **C.** Choice C lists the correct order for the layers of skin from the innermost (deep) to the outermost (superficial) layer: hypodermis, dermis, epidermis. The innermost layer of the skin is the hypodermis (subcutaneous) that contains mostly adipose tissue. (Below that you would find muscle, bone, and organs.) The middle layer of the skin is the dermis. The layer of skin we see is the epidermis, the outermost (superficial) layer.

8. **C.** Sarcomeres, choice C, make up the repeated sequence of myosin and actin, which gives skeletal muscle a striated appearance. Muscle fibers certainly exist in other types of muscle, but they are not arranged into sarcomeres, the *repeated* sequencing. Myocardium (choice A), heart muscle, is not a type of skeletal muscle. Endomysium (choice B) is the connective tissue that encapsulates a single muscle cell; it does not give a striated appearance. Myocytes or muscle cells contain numerous mitochondria (choice D) to give energy to the muscle, but this is not what gives it the striated appearance.

9. **D.** Glucagon, choice D, is a hormone released by the pancreas when blood sugar levels are low. Glucagon causes the liver to release glucose through a metabolic pathway called gluconeogenesis (choice A). Adrenalin (choice B) is released by the adrenal glands during certain body states, such as the fight-or-flight response. Adrenalin actually does cause blood sugar to increase, something you will learn more about in nursing school, but this is not the primary corrective pathway the human body uses when blood glucose is low. Insulin (choice C) has the opposite effect of glucagon, a decrease in blood glucose; however, both are released by the kidneys.

10. **A.** After the blood arrives back to the heart from the superior and inferior vena cava, the blood spills into the right atria, choice A. From the right atria, the blood moves to the right ventricle (choice B), the lungs, the left atria (choice C), the left ventricle (choice D), and then the systemic body. This is a fairly easy question, but you must know the names of where the blood is flowing, including the pulmonary vessels.

11. **B.** An ECG/EKG shows the healthcare provider the electrical activity of the heart, choice B. In a normal heart this electrical activity comes from the sinoatrial (SA) node, but this is not always the case. One thing is certain, however: The electrical impulse always comes before the contraction of the heart (systolic and diastolic contractions, choice A). Myocardial movement (choice C) is the same thing as a systolic and diastolic contraction. There are receptors in the aorta (choice D) that sense blood pressure, but this is unrelated to reading an ECG/EKG.

12. **A.** The alimentary canal is another term for the gastrointestinal tract, but this does not include the organs utilized by the digestive system as a whole. The liver, choice A, is one such organ. Others include the pancreas and gallbladder. They are a part of the digestive system, but *not* part of the alimentary canal. The esophagus (choice B), rectum (choice C), and jejunum (choice D) are parts of the alimentary canal.

13. **A.** Carbon dioxide, choice A, is typically converted to bicarbonate and causes the creation of hydrogen. This action has a direct influence on the pH of the blood. You will learn more about blood pH in nursing school; for the time being, simply understand that carbon dioxide and hydrogen influence pH. Oxygen (choice B) does not influence pH, nor does carbon monoxide (choice C). Nitrogen (choice D) makes up the majority of air, but it does not influence blood pH.

14. **B.** Hydrostatic pressure is a fancy way of saying blood pressure, choice B. For the purpose of preparing for the HESI A2, this point should not become more complicated than that. The Latin term "hydro" means water, or fluid in this sense. The term "static" means to weigh, or in this case the pressure. The filtration through the kidneys occurs because the heart pumps blood and pushes it through the renal artery and into the nephrons. Osmotic pressure (choice A) does play a role in blood filtration in the glomerulus, but it is not the main force; it would be considered a sister concept to hydrostatic pressure. Concentration pressure (choice C) is the natural movement of molecules via diffusion or osmosis. Venous pressure (choice D) describes the pressure inside the venous system; this would be after blood is filtered through the kidneys and is returning to the heart.

15. **C.** Cerumen, or ear wax, is released by sudoriferous (sweat) glands in the ears, choice C. The skin (choice A) also has sudoriferous glands; however, they release sweat, not cerumen. The mouth (choice B) hosts the salivary glands, the largest of which are the parotid glands. The eyes (choice D) host glands that release tears and oils.

16. **B.** Bone, choice B, has the highest concentration of calcium in the body. Osteoblasts form new bone and deposit the calcium. Cartilage (choice A) is a type of connective tissue, but it is flexible and not composed of calcium. Tendons (choice C), like cartilage and bone, are a type of connective tissue; however, tendons are made up of mostly collagen. Blood (choice D) does in fact carry calcium. It is also considered a vascular connective tissue. Calcium is not a major component of blood, however, and is not mineralized.

17. **C.** When injured and bleeding, the body wants to return to homeostasis and stop bleeding. It will accomplish that through a positive feedback loop, choice C. A feedback loop is either positive or negative; it is not variable (choice B). A positive feedback loop is a pathway within the body where the condition causes an increase in the process. A negative feedback loop (choice D) has the opposite effect. An abnormal condition would cause a reaction to fix it, such as the release of insulin in response to high blood sugar. Homeostasis (choice A) is the balance at which our bodies function best: normal or baseline.

18. **A.** The medulla oblongata, choice A, is found in the brainstem and is largely responsible for a constant heart rate and breathing. The hypothalamus (choice B) plays an important role in regulating the pituitary gland. It also regulates body temperature and emotions, among other things. The cerebellum (choice C) aids in balance and coordination. The cerebrum (choice D) is the large football-shaped area of the brain that contains the many lobes from frontal to occipital.

19. **B.** The thyroid gland is most commonly known to regulate metabolism, choice B. A small organ at the bottom of our neck, it interacts with multiple organs of the body. Calcium (choice A) is regulated by the parathyroid gland. Insulin and glucagon (choice C) are regulated by the pancreas. The fight-or-flight response (choice D) is regulated by the adrenal glands with the release of adrenalin.

20. **A.** Sensory neurons, choice A, capture the senses you feel, such as pain when placing your hand on a hot stove. This can include anything from pain (nociceptors) to temperature (thermoreceptors). They are all types of sensory neurons that send signals back to the brain so the human body may be aware and respond. Motor neurons (choice B) work for the movement of our muscles. Reflex neuron (choice C) is not appropriate terminology; however, reflex arcs exist, such as a knee jerk when tapped with a hammer. A key feature of a reflex arc is that it does not initially reach the brain; instead, the body reacts as a reflex. This can occur with pain as well, but again, the signal would not reach the brain to react. Association neurons (choice D), also known as interneurons, are the most common neurons in the body; they transmit sensory and motor signals.

21. **B.** The chondrocyte, choice B, is a specialized cell that builds the connective tissue matrix of cartilage. Osteoblasts (choice A) build bone. Erythrocytes (choice C) are red blood cells; remember, they do not have a nucleus. Melanocytes (choice D) are cells that give our skin its color or pigment.

22. **D.** Creatinine and urea, choice D, are waste products excreted by the kidneys. Creatinine is a waste product created by normal muscle function. Urea is created by normal body metabolism. Antidiuretic hormone (ADH; choice A) stimulates the body to hold onto more water. It is a hormone, not a waste product. Water and sodium (choice B) are certainly excreted by the kidneys; however, they would not be considered waste products. The body needs water and sodium; the vast majority is reabsorbed in the renal tubules. Bile is excreted through stool, and ammonia can be excreted via stool or kidneys, eliminating choice C.

23. **A.** Oogenesis, choice A, is the creation of eggs in a female; it occurs in the ovaries and begins while the female baby is still in the womb of her mother. Oogenesis does not occur in the liver (choice B), pancreas (choice C), or brain (choice D). It is helpful to recognize that "genesis" means the creation of something. For example, gluconeogenesis is the creation of glucose.

24. **D.** A frontal plane, choice D, also called a coronal plane, divides into anterior and posterior portions. A transverse plane (choice C) divides into superior and inferior portions; it can also be called a horizontal plane (choice A). A sagittal plane (choice B) divides into right and left portions.

25. **A.** Tight junctions, choice A, cause the membranes to be incredibly selective, only allowing certain things to pass through. Any large molecules will not make it past. High blood pressure (choice B) would be a bad thing to have anywhere in the body; it is not a protective measure. Small capillaries (choice C) do exist in the brain, but protecting the brain from unwanted pathogens is not related to the size of the capillaries. Cerebrospinal fluid (CSF; choice D) delivers nutrients or waste; it also protects the brain and spinal cord, but it does not affect the blood-brain barrier. For future knowledge, when CSF becomes infected, this can often lead to meningitis.

Resource Materials

Temperature Scales

The United States utilizes the Fahrenheit scale. Nearly every other country, however, does not. Celsius, also called centigrade, is the most widely used scale for science, and for the rest of the world.

Fahrenheit

- 98.6° F: Normal body temperature
- 32° F: Water freezes
- Expressed in degrees

Celsius

- 37° C: Normal body temperature
- 0° C: Water freezes
- Expressed in degrees

Kelvin

- 0 K: Absolute zero
- Not expressed in degrees

The Metric System

Below are the most common metric units of measurement used by healthcare workers.

Prefix	Abbreviation	Exponential
kilo	k	10^3
centi	c	10^{-2}
milli	m	10^{-3}
micro	μ	10^{-6}

HESI Tip: Kilogram is commonly used for patient weight. Centimeter is commonly used for patient height. Milligram and microgram are commonly used as dosages for medications.

Conversions

- 1 kg = 2.2 lb
- 30 mL = 1 oz
- 1 mL = 1 cc

Multiples of Ten

The metric system functions on multiples of 10. This makes the system very easy to use. Simply move the decimal place to the left or right.

- 1 g = 1000 mg
- 1 mg = 1000 mcg
- 1 L = 1000 mL

Metric Units	Conversion
Length	
Millimeter (mm)	$1\,mm = 0.1\,cm = \dfrac{1}{10}\,cm$ $1\,mm = 0.001\,m = \dfrac{1}{1000}\,m$
Centimeter (cm)	$1\,cm = 10\,mm$ $1\,cm = 0.01\,m = \dfrac{1}{100}\,m$
Meter (m)	$1\,m = 1000\,mm$ $1\,m = 100\,cm$ $1\,m = 0.001\,km = \dfrac{1}{1000}\,km$
Kilometer (km)	$1\,km = 1000\,m$
Mass	
Milligram (mg)	$1\,mg = 0.001\,g = \dfrac{1}{1000}\,g$
Gram (g)	$1\,g = 1000\,mg$ $1\,g = 0.001\,kg = \dfrac{1}{1000}\,kg$
Kilogram (kg)	$1\,kg = 1000\,g$
Capacity	
Milliliter (mL)	$1\,mL = 0.001\,L = \dfrac{1}{1000}\,L$
Liter (L)	$1\,L = 1000\,mL$

International System of Units (SI)

Science topics in general utilize the International System of Units (SI). While the United States as a whole has not adopted SI units or the metric system, it is the favored system of measurement in scientific and medical communities. Below is an overview of the units with their associated symbol.

Base Units

Simple Single Unit Measurements		
Unit	Symbol	Definition
second	s	time
meter	m	length
kilogram	kg	mass
ampere	A	electric current

Derived Units

Derived Units		
Unit	Symbol	Definition
newton	N	force
radian	rad	plane angle
joule	J	energy
hertz	Hz	frequency
watt	W	power
coulomb	C	electric charge
volt	V	voltage
ohm	Ω	resistance

The Periodic Table

PERIODIC TABLE OF THE ELEMENTS

1	2	3	4	5	6	7	8	9	10	11	12	13	14	15	16	17	18
1 **H** 1.008																	2 **He** 4.00
3 **Li** 6.94	4 **Be** 9.01											5 **B** 10.81	6 **C** 12.01	7 **N** 14.01	8 **O** 16.00	9 **F** 19.00	10 **Ne** 20.18
11 **Na** 22.99	12 **Mg** 24.30											13 **Al** 26.98	14 **Si** 28.09	15 **P** 30.97	16 **S** 32.06	17 **Cl** 35.45	18 **Ar** 39.95
19 **K** 39.10	20 **Ca** 40.08	21 **Sc** 44.96	22 **Ti** 47.90	23 **V** 50.94	24 **Cr** 52.00	25 **Mn** 54.94	26 **Fe** 55.85	27 **Co** 58.93	28 **Ni** 58.69	29 **Cu** 63.55	30 **Zn** 65.39	31 **Ga** 69.72	32 **Ge** 72.59	33 **As** 74.92	34 **Se** 78.96	35 **Br** 79.90	36 **Kr** 83.80
37 **Rb** 85.47	38 **Sr** 87.62	39 **Y** 88.91	40 **Zr** 91.22	41 **Nb** 92.91	42 **Mo** 95.94	43 **Tc** (98)	44 **Ru** 101.1	45 **Rh** 102.91	46 **Pd** 106.42	47 **Ag** 107.87	48 **Cd** 112.41	49 **In** 114.82	50 **Sn** 118.71	51 **Sb** 121.75	52 **Te** 127.60	53 **I** 126.91	54 **Xe** 131.29
55 **Cs** 132.91	56 **Ba** 137.33	57 ***La** 138.91	72 **Hf** 178.49	73 **Ta** 180.95	74 **W** 183.85	75 **Re** 186.21	76 **Os** 190.2	77 **Ir** 192.2	78 **Pt** 195.08	79 **Au** 196.97	80 **Hg** 200.59	81 **Tl** 204.38	82 **Pb** 207.2	83 **Bi** 208.98	84 **Po** (209)	85 **At** (210)	86 **Rn** (222)
87 **Fr** (223)	88 **Ra** 226.02	89 **†Ac** 227.03	104 **Rf** (261)	105 **Db** (262)	106 **Sg** (266)	107 **Bh** (264)	108 **Hs** (277)	109 **Mt** (268)	110 **Ds** (271)	111 **Rg** (272)							

*Lanthanide Series

58 **Ce** 140.12	59 **Pr** 140.91	60 **Nd** 144.24	61 **Pm** (145)	62 **Sm** 150.4	63 **Eu** 151.97	64 **Gd** 157.25	65 **Tb** 158.93	66 **Dy** 162.50	67 **Ho** 164.93	68 **Er** 167.26	69 **Tm** 168.93	70 **Yb** 173.04	71 **Lu** 174.97

†Actinide Series

90 **Tn** 232.04	91 **Pa** 231.04	92 **U** 238.03	93 **Np** (237)	94 **Pu** (244)	95 **Am** (243)	96 **Cm** (247)	97 **Bk** (247)	98 **Cf** (251)	99 **Es** (252)	100 **Fm** (257)	101 **Md** (258)	102 **No** (259)	103 **Lr** (262)